Foreword by Richard DuFour

Pyramid Response to Intervention

RTI, Professional Learning Communities, and How to Respond When Kids Don't Learn

Austin Buffum

Mike Mattos

Chris Weber

Solution Tree | Press

a division of

Solution Tree

555 North Morton Street
Bloomington, IN 47404
800.733.6786 (toll free) / 812.336.7700
FAX: 812.336.7790

email: info@solution-tree.com
solution-tree.com

Printed in the United States of America

FSC
Mixed Sources
Product group from well-managed
forests and other controlled sources

Cert no. SW-COC-002283
www.fsc.org
© 1996 Forest Stewardship Council

ISBN 978-1-934009-33-8

To Dr. Harold E. Hester and Mr. Richard Johnson,
great educators and even greater friends

—Austin Buffum

To Anita and Laurel, who inspire every aspect of my life

—Mike Mattos

To my wife and daughters—Pamela, Sophie, and Chloe

—Chris Weber

Acknowledgments

$\mathcal{W}$e want to first acknowledge the many great colleagues with whom we have had the pleasure to work and who have made a real difference in the lives of countless children—specifically, the exceptional staffs of Marjorie Veeh and Richard Henry Dana Elementary Schools, Pioneer Middle School, and the Education Division of the Capistrano Unified School District. Many of the proven practices described in this book have been created through the collaborative efforts of these dedicated educators.

We further wish to acknowledge the support and guidance we have received from the outstanding staff at Solution Tree. President Jeff Jones, our editor Gretchen Knapp, and the professional development team have created an environment of integrity and trust in which our efforts have been nurtured and informed. In a day and age where most of corporate America is driven by profits and the bottom line, we are honored to work with a company that is singularly focused on the noble pursuit of improving schools across the United States and Canada.

We also want to acknowledge and thank our fellow PLC Associates who continue to work across North America in support of our commonly held belief that it is our job to ensure high levels of learning for all students.

Finally, we want to sincerely thank Rick DuFour, Becky DuFour, and Bob Eaker (the three Rs), who inspire our passion for education and from whom we continue to learn. Their collective wisdom has deeply impacted every aspect of our professional beliefs and practices, and their support and friendship have indelibly enriched our lives. We truly feel that in regards to these three, we must echo the words of Sir Isaac Newton, who in 1676 said, "If I have seen further, it is by standing on the shoulders of giants."

Visit **go.solution-tree.com/rti**
to download all of the reproducibles
in this book.

Table of Contents

Chapter Four

Laying the Foundation: A Professional Learning Community 47

Chapter Five

Learning CPR 59

About the Authors

Austin Buffum

*A*ustin Buffum, Ed.D., is retired as the senior deputy superintendent of the Capistrano Unified School District, which serves more than 51,000 students in South Orange County, California. For his excellent leadership, Dr. Buffum was selected 2006 Curriculum and Instruction Administrator of the Year by the Association of California School Administrators. During his 37-year career in public education, Dr. Buffum also served as a music teacher and coordinator, elementary school principal, curriculum director, and assistant superintendent. In addition to articles published in the *Journal of Staff Development, American School Board Journal, and Leadership,* he contributed a chapter, "Trust. The Secret Ingredient to Successful Shared Leadership," to *The Collaborative Administrator* (Solution Tree, 2008). He shares his in-depth knowledge of building and sustaining PLCs with schools, districts, and state departments of education throughout North America.

Mike Mattos

*T*he leadership of Mike Mattos, M.S., principal of Pioneer Middle School in Tustin, California, has resulted in consistently outstanding student achievement. Pioneer was named a California Distinguished School in 2003 and 2007, and was one of only eight schools in the nation featured in the professional development video series *The Power of Professional Learning Communities at Work™: Bringing the Big Ideas to Life.* Previously, as principal of Marjorie Veeh Elementary School in Tustin, Mike helped create a powerful professional learning community; in 2004, Veeh was one of only 18 California elementary schools to be named both a California Distinguished School and a National Title I Achieving School.

Mike's chapter "Walk the 'Lign: Aligning School Practices With Essential PLC Characteristics" appeared in *The Collaborative Administrator*, and he contributed to *Revisiting Professional Learning Communities at Work™: New Insights for Improving Schools* (DuFour, DuFour, & Eaker, 2008). Mike is a nationally recognized presenter and consultant, sharing his knowledge with educators throughout North America.

Chris Weber

Chris Weber, Ed.D., has been a teacher at all grade levels, from kindergarten through 12th grade, and an administrator at the elementary and secondary school levels. The former principal of Richard Henry Dana Elementary School in Dana Point, California, he now serves as Director of K–6 Instructional Services in Garden Grove Unified School District in Orange County, California. Dr. Weber is a former Air Force pilot and a graduate of the U.S. Air Force Academy.

Foreword

Schools and districts throughout the United States are confronting the challenge of responding to the legislative initiative known as *response to intervention* or RTI. Educators in traditional schools will regard this legislation as yet another imposition, an intrusion into their practice and an interruption of their real work. Educators in these schools are prone to regard virtually any task that calls for a coordinated and collective effort—engaging in the accreditation process, creating new curriculum or assessments, developing and achieving school goals, analyzing evidence of student learning as part of a continuous improvement process—as an annoying departure from their day-to-day labors. Inevitably, they respond to these intrusions with a spirit of compliance rather than a spirit of commitment and thus are able to minimize the impact of improvement initiatives.

The reason for their conditioned response is simple: In most schools, the work of educators is done in isolation. As a result, any task that requires a collaborative effort is considered a burden, an annoying add-on to the already too-full agendas of individual teachers working in isolation.

There are other schools, however, whose educators will integrate the RTI initiative into their existing, well-defined improvement processes and use it as a catalyst for enhancing both student and adult learning. Working collaboratively, learning together rather than in isolation, creating systematic responses to address problems, and using evidence of student learning to drive continuous improvement are deeply embedded in the culture of these schools. Most importantly, educators in these schools acknowledge and embrace a shared purpose of helping all students learn at high levels and take collective responsibility for achieving that shared purpose. In these schools, RTI will reinforce and strengthen the assumptions, commitments, and practices that already exist, and educators will work together to implement, assess, and improve the model.

The power of *Pyramid Response to Intervention* is that the authors have led such exemplary schools and districts. They "get it." They have the insights and deep understanding of school improvement that can only come from learning by doing. They have been immersed in the real world of schools, and they know that programs don't improve schools—people do. They understand that although it is easy for educators to create new structures—policies, programs, and procedures—it is difficult for them to change traditional school cultures—the assumptions, expectations, beliefs, and habits that constitute the norm. They understand that if schools are to become more effective in helping all students learn at high levels, RTI must represent only one aspect of the deep cultural change that must occur. Perhaps most importantly, they believe in the very real possibility of transforming a school's culture because they have been spectacularly successful in leading that transformation themselves.

I have the highest regard for Austin Buffum, Mike Mattos, and Chris Weber. The wisdom and insights of these award-winning educators represent a major contribution to the field of education. I have no doubt that scores of books and articles will be written advising educators as to how they should implement the RTI initiative in their schools and districts. Most of those books will explain the intricacies of the law, clarify terms, and offer different models for consideration. If, however, educators merely add RTI as an appendage to traditional school cultures or consider it a "special education" issue, there is no reason to believe schools will be any more successful in their efforts to help all students learn.

This book, however, is not about responding to legislative initiatives or implementing new programs. It is, above all, a book to transform schools, a book that not only calls on educators to improve their schools but also gives them the information, processes, and tools essential to that work. I highly recommend it to all those interested in making schools better places for student and adult learning.

—Richard DuFour

Preface

Dear God, be good to me;
The sea is so wide,
And my boat is so small.

—Breton Fisherman's Prayer

*I*n the autumn of 1991, a powerful, enormous storm formed in the Atlantic Ocean; it was later called the "perfect storm" because it could not have been more intense. The storm began to form when a cold front moved along the U.S.–Canadian border. Its leading edge over Indiana in the Midwest contained a pocket of low barometric pressure called a short-wave trough at about 20,000 feet (Junger, 1997). It moved toward the East at about 40 miles per hour until it reached Maine, where it then proceeded out into the Atlantic and combined with another trough full of warm air that was quickly rising.

At the same time, a large high-pressure system was beginning to form over the Canadian coast. When the cold front met with this high-pressure system in the North Atlantic, it created an even larger storm. However, there was yet another factor. Hurricane Grace, in its final phase, moved into the same region from the south, bringing warm air from the Caribbean that fed more intense energy into the storm over the Atlantic.

Together these storms created one megastorm, the likes of which had not been seen in over a century. The megastorm blew back and forth across the North Atlantic for a week, with winds over 150 mph that kicked up waves over 50 feet tall. The Air National Guard rescued many boats caught at the edges of the storm, including one fishing boat that became the subject of a Hollywood movie, appropriately titled *The Perfect Storm*, based upon Sebastian Junger's 1997 book of the same name.

This perfect storm was caused by the combination of meteorological circumstances that had never been seen before. A dying hurricane, a high-pressure system, and a cold front combined to produce unparalleled devastation. We recount this story because another unique set of circumstances—educational, economic, and demographic—is building in the United States that may have equally devastating results upon our country and its people.

According to the Policy Evaluation and Research Center (Kirsch, Braun, Yamamoto, & Sum, 2007), three forces are converging to create this perfect storm that affects America's future: the wide disparity in literacy and numeracy skills among our school-age and adult population, economic forces (particularly technology and globalization) that have produced a labor market very different from those of earlier decades, and sweeping demographic changes that will result in an increasingly older and more diverse America. Surveys of American adults (Kirsch, Jungeblut, Jenkins, & Kolstad, 1993) reveal that more than 50% of Americans lack the necessary literacy and math skills to participate fully in the current competitive and technologically advanced job market. Moreover, these skills are not evenly distributed across groups defined by race, ethnicity, country of birth, or socioeconomic status; for some groups, the literacy and numeracy gap is so great that it affects their members' social, educational, and economic opportunities.

Technology and globalization have changed the face of the workplace in America. The automobile industry is one example of this, as robots and computers have taken jobs that once were held by high-skilled laborers. Another example is the textile industry, which can send raw materials to the other side of the globe, use the cheap labor in faraway countries to manufacture their products, and then sell them at retail price, without having to pay the higher wages of American unionized labor.

Simultaneously, our population is becoming more diverse. Immigration to the United States has increased rapidly since the late 1980s. Between 2000 and 2005, two thirds of U.S. labor force growth and 86% of net employment growth have been created by new immigrants (U.S. Census Bureau, 2008, as cited in Kirsch et al., 2007). Naturally, immigrant students are not as proficient on literacy tests as students who were born in America; many of them are unable to speak English when they enter school. On the 1995 International Adult Literacy Survey, immigrants' average proficiency scores on three separate literacy scales were more than one standard deviation lower than nonimmigrants (Sum, Kirsch, & Yamamoto, 2004).

If we do not change our thinking about the status of public education, the United States could continue to lose ground economically to the rest of the world. Former Secretary of the Treasury Robert Rubin (2006) has argued that for Americans to achieve a more widely shared prosperity, "broad participation in economic well-being and growth is critical, both as a fundamental value and to realize our economic potential" (p. A-20). We must decide whether we will allow ourselves to become more fractured socially and economically, or whether we will invest in ideas to bring us together. Unless America's perfect storm in education is quelled soon, it will only accelerate the current dividing process and thus put the American dream in jeopardy for large numbers of people. America's long-held belief in individual ambition leading inevitably toward success, as in the tales of Horatio Alger, may be giving way to a society in which class and privilege correlate more directly with success than do effort and ambition.

This book offers hope to America's schools. We believe that educators can quell this storm by turning away from the threats and intimidation of the No Child Left Behind mandates and by focusing instead upon four key questions of the professional learning community:

1. What exactly do we expect all students to learn?

2. How will we know if and when they've learned it?

3. How will we respond when some students don't learn?

4. How will we respond when some students have already learned? (DuFour, DuFour, Eaker, & Many, 2006)

We will focus on answering Question 3 in light of federal legislation and the Individuals with Disabilities Education Improvement Act of 2004 (IDEIA), particularly its proposal for response to intervention initiatives.

But more importantly, we deeply believe that it is imperative to the future of our nation that we strengthen our schools, empower our teachers, and fight to ensure high levels of learning for all students. We humbly hope that this book may, in some way, help schools to weather the perfect storm.

Chapter One
What Is Pyramid Response to Intervention?

The only source of knowledge is experience.

—Albert Einstein

*T*his book is written for practitioners by practitioners. As authors, we represent three different generations of public school educators—a Baby Boomer, a Gen-Xer, and a Millennial—with over 75 years of combined experience in working with children and their parents. Each of us has implemented professional learning communities in our schools and districts. Each of us believes deeply in the power of collaboration and the goal of continuous improvement, and we've struggled to find increasingly better answers to the question, "How do we respond when students don't learn?" Woven throughout this book are stories of real schools that have also been seeking better answers. Narrative case studies that open each chapter show how various responses play out at the school, classroom, and individual student levels. We believe that educators should always consider our actions' impact upon individual students, not just upon the average scores that comprise a school's collective adequate yearly progress. As practitioners in our own schools and districts, the three of us have witnessed firsthand the power of timely, systematic interventions on student learning. This book explores two closely related ideas, response to intervention (RTI) and the pyramid of interventions (POI), that we believe benefit educators at every level in finding new ways to help every child be successful.

Response to Intervention (RTI)

Einstein once defined insanity as "doing the same thing over and over again and expecting different results." In this spirit, for 30 years, American schools used a *discrepancy model* to determine whether a struggling child would receive additional time and support through special education. The discrepancy model measures the difference between a child's potential and actual achievement to determine whether the child has a learning disability. The problem with this system, of course, is that no action can take place until there is a discrepancy—until the child has already failed. Under this system, as John McCook (2006, p. 1) comments, "It must be the child's fault, or the problem certainly must be the child. Why else would the child have such a discrepancy between expected achievement and actual achievement?"

Response to intervention (RTI) is a new movement that shifts the responsibility for helping all students become successful from the special education teachers and curriculum to the entire staff, including special *and* regular education teachers and curriculum. This seismic shift in educational policy culminated in the Individuals with Disabilities Education Improvement Act (IDEIA), which was signed into law by President George W. Bush in December 2004.

Brown-Chidsey and Steege (2005) observe, "What makes RTI different from . . . prior means of helping students is that . . . assessment and instruction practices are integrated into an objectives-based system with built-in decision stages" (p. x). An RTI system promises more than an alternative way for qualifying students to receive special services; it promises (and may in fact require) a unified system of education (Faust, 2006). In this unified system, assessment—universal, ongoing, and formative—assumes an increasingly important role in classrooms and schools. A team of experts will use a systemic approach to implement programs with *fidelity*—the way they were intended and designed.

Human resources (including classroom teachers, speech and language pathologists, psychologists and social workers, special education teachers, and administrators) will be deployed in new ways to collectively assist all students. New academic resources will be sought out, evaluated, and implemented with individuals and groups of students more often and with greater diagnostic specificity than they have in the past. Schools will provide flexible support to students by modifying the frequency and types of assistance.

While components of RTI had been around for years (and were widely developed at Adlai Stevenson High School, as we shall see in the next section), schools traditionally limited its use to special education classrooms. Today this approach centers on the regular classroom teacher:

> Notwithstanding section 607(b), when determining whether a child has a specific learning disability as defined in section 602(29), a local education agency shall not be required to take into consideration whether a child has a severe discrepancy between achievement and intellectual ability. . . . In determining whether a child has a specific learning disability, a local educational agency may use a process that determines if the child responds to a scientific, research-based intervention as part of the evaluation procedures. {IDEIA, 2004, Section 614(b)(6)(A & B)}

Simply put, under RTI, schools will consider most students for special education services only after the students have not responded to a series of timely, systematic, increasingly focused, and intensive research-based interventions, which are the responsibility of the regular education program. This is a seismic and explicit change from the discrepancy model. Federal regulations argue:

> There are many reasons why the use of the IQ-discrepancy criterion should be abandoned. The IQ discrepancy criterion is potentially harmful to students as it results in delaying intervention until the student's achievement is sufficiently low so that the discrepancy is achieved. (U.S. Department of Education, 2005, p. 35802)

The phrase *potentially harmful* seems to imply that schools that continue to wait for students to fail in order to qualify them to receive additional services might find themselves in jeopardy of legal action by the families of students with special needs.

There are viable alternatives to the discrepancy model. While some researchers and educators were developing the theories and practices that led to the creation of RTI as envisioned in IDEIA, others were simultaneously considering the question, "How does our school respond when we discover that some children are not learning?" These educators, following the professional learning communities model of Richard DuFour, Robert Eaker, and Rebecca DuFour, created a tiered system of interventions graphically represented by a pyramid: the pyramid of interventions.

Pyramid of Interventions (POI)

Adlai Stevenson High School in suburban Chicago was practicing something very like RTI long before it was written into law. Stevenson is one of three schools in the nation to have received the U.S. Department of Education Blue Ribbon award on four separate occasions. It is a model of continuous improvement that veteran educational consultant and author Mike Schmoker (2001) has recognized as "an undeniably world-class school" (p. 31).

Yet in 1983, the staff at Stevenson realized that although many of its students were successful because of the faculty's hard work, more than 25% "had been relegated to remedial curricular tracks and, at the end of each semester, teachers were recommending that hundreds of students be transferred to a lower track" (DuFour, DuFour, Eaker, & Karhanek, 2004, p. 44). In discussing this challenge, Stevenson teachers focused on the reality that the incoming students lacked the necessary study skills and work habits, and that simply allowing them to fail did not seem to motivate students to change their behaviors. The faculty came to realize that they were doing an outstanding job of giving students the *opportunity* to learn: "But, to the enduring credit of Stevenson's wonderful faculty, they did not settle for giving students the chance to learn. Instead, they began a systematic effort to better meet the needs of all students so that the school's promise of 'success for all' might be a reality rather than a slogan" (DuFour et al., 2004, p. 47).

This effort led to what has become known as the *pyramid of interventions* (POI), a collective and systematic approach to providing additional time and support to students who experience difficulties in learning.

A Vision of the Future

When schools operate as professional learning communities, create a pyramid of interventions, and implement response to intervention, they create the opportunity for powerful change. We believe these three ideas will unite the long-separated worlds of regular education and special education to create a unified system of schooling. With the demise of the "wait-to-fail" model, we can now move toward a systematic, directive, and timely response to all children when they don't learn adequately, regardless of labels or subgroups.

Pyramid Response to Intervention (PRTI)

Although we are hesitant to invent another educational acronym, we need a term to help educators understand that the POI developed at Stevenson High School and the RTI approach prescribed in IDEIA 2004 are almost the same system. Each brings its own unique strengths, and together they create a synergy that we believe will be superior to either system used alone.

Both POI and RTI demand that we address the culture of our schools rather than simply adding new structures—that we make a cultural shift to ensure that all staff members demonstrate a collective responsibility to help all students learn. Both are based on the premise that some students need more time and support to ensure their learning. Both encourage educators not to wait until students possess the correct label to provide this support, lest students fall so far behind that they can never catch up. Both provide a systematic process of intervention that is implemented schoolwide, rather than varying teacher to teacher. Both provide academic *and* behavioral interventions—academic interventions for those who *can't* learn, behavioral interventions for those who *won't* learn. (Behavioral interventions are described in detail in chapter 9.) Finally, both ideas utilize a system of interventions that are increasingly more intensive and directive, and both are commonly represented visually by pyramids with three tiers (see Figure 1-1, page 6).

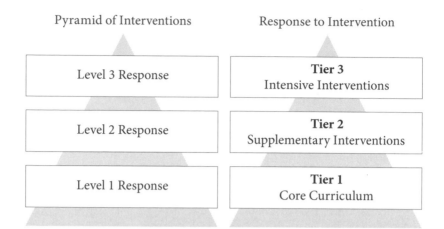

**Figure 1-1: A comparison of the pyramid of interventions
and response to intervention models**

Chapters 2, 3, and 4 will go into more depth on the individual characteristics of RTI and POI. In this chapter, we'll explore how PRTI pulls the best from both. From response to intervention, PRTI takes its structure, its approach to universal screening and progress monitoring, and its requirement for research-based interventions. From the pyramid of interventions, PRTI takes its culture; its philosophy of timely, directive, systemic, flexible support; and its process for creating and supporting shared instructional goals.

Structure

The base of the PLC pyramid of interventions describes *the initial interventions* we implement when some students don't learn what we have defined as "essential." By contrast, the base of the RTI pyramid describes *the core program* that 100% of the students receive. While the first two critical questions of the professional learning community ("What exactly do we expect all students to learn?" and "How will we know if they've learned it?" [DuFour et al., 2006]) help to define and ensure a guaranteed, viable core curriculum, the PLC pyramid has not typically depicted Tier 1 as the core program.

Universal Screening

RTI encourages us to use universal screening tools in both academics *and* behavior even before the school year has begun to identify students who need additional time and support. Some professional learning communities already employ some universal screening measures, such as the Counselor Watch program at Adlai Stevenson High School. However, under RTI, schools are encouraged 1) to apply universal screening in a broader context that includes behavior as well as literacy and numeracy skills, and 2) to explicitly base decisions upon highly specific data.

Frequent Progress Monitoring

Though both POI and RTI emphasize progress monitoring to measure the effectiveness of an intervention overall and for individual students, they differ in the intensity required. Schools implementing POI gather timely, frequent information on student achievement through common formative assessments, but RTI's increased emphasis on progress monitoring might mean monitoring student progress as often as twice each week, using very short, specific probes to detect small changes in student learning. This kind of intense monitoring of students is probably more frequent than most professional learning communities use as part of a pyramid of interventions.

Research-Based Interventions

While the PLC pyramid certainly has no bias against interventions that have a research base, RTI legislation (IDEIA, 2004) places a greater emphasis on the use of *scientific, research-based interventions,* defined by the No Child Left Behind Act (2001) as "research that involves the application of rigorous, systematic, and objective procedures to obtain reliable and valid knowledge relevant to education activities and programs" {20 USC 6312(c)(1)(F); 20 USC 6612(b)(1)}.

School Culture

PRTI also draws on the unique strengths of the professional learning communities model. PRTI schools often must modify their master schedules or "the way we do things around here" so as to provide systematic interventions during the regular school day, without forcing students to miss core instruction in the regular classroom. In addition, PRTI encourages teachers and administrators alike to "think outside of the box," so as to provide these guaranteed interventions without hiring new staff or spending more money as a prerequisite to action. Once a professional learning community has found a way to provide students this additional time and support, the staff "brainstorms" a series of interventions. Though schools with significant subgroups often focus on the needs of those students to the exclusion of other students who do not belong to any identifiable subgroup, a professional learning community guarantees that no student is left behind.

Timely, Directive, Systemic, Flexible Support

As in the pyramid of interventions, in PRTI, students receive *timely* interventions at the first indication that they need more time and support. This process should be *directive* rather than invitational, so that students get the extra help they need, consistently and without interruption *until they are successful.* Finally, this extra support should not be dependent upon which teacher the student has, but instead should be implemented systemically, so that every student who faces the same problem is guaranteed the same response.

Interventions are sequenced to build upon each other, from least to most restrictive, from least to most intensive, and from what happens in every classroom for all children to what happens for individual students who need highly focused, targeted help (see Figure 1-2, page 9). The system of interventions is flexible and emphasizes returning students to the regular instructional program as quickly as possible; students receive interventions only when needed and for the particular subject in which they need assistance.

Shared Instructional Goals

As noted earlier, RTI requires very frequent progress monitoring. This practice, though more intense in RTI, is not entirely new to a professional learning community. A PLC relies upon frequent, timely, common formative assessment data to determine which students need additional time and support, not last year's summative assessment data. The RTI emphasis on progress monitoring will not be effective, however, if educators have not first collaborated to identify common instructional goals. Educators begin the PRTI process by working together in teams to answer the first two questions of a professional learning community: "What do we want students to know and be able to do *this* year?" and "How will we know if and when they've learned it?" The team then modifies or replaces

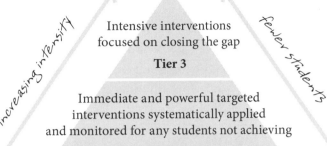

Increasing intensity

fewer students

Intensive interventions
focused on closing the gap

Tier 3

Immediate and powerful targeted
interventions systematically applied
and monitored for any students not achieving

Tier 2

A coherent and viable core curriculum that embeds
ongoing monitoring for all students

Tier 1

A Focus on Learning • A Collaborative Culture • A Focus on Results

Figure 1-2: The pyramid response to intervention model

interventions when assessments indicate that they are not successful or
when the team discovers a more powerful intervention.

Thus, pyramid response to intervention combines the regulatory
requirements of response to intervention with the time-proven effectiveness
of the pyramid of interventions. PRTI uses the well-established power of
the professional learning community model to drive the structural and
procedural practices of response to intervention.

The Right Work at the Right Time

We believe that American public education is on the precipice of
dramatic positive change. PRTI does not merely address learning outcomes
for special education students; it integrates "special education" and
"regular education" into simply "education." PRTI brings together all staff
to improve learning by delivering effective instruction and interventions
to all students, without first waiting for them to fail. Adopting PRTI is
about using best professional practice and insisting that we do what is best,
necessary, and right for all students—the right work at the right time.

We wish to reassure schools that already have begun their PLC journey
that implementing PRTI will *not* be just another "new thing." With a

few caveats (such as the need for scientific, research-based interventions; universal screening; and progress monitoring), PRTI involves the same work as answering the PLC question, "How will we respond when kids don't learn?" For those practitioners who have not yet begun the PLC journey, we will make the case that the most promising and research-supported way to implement response to intervention is to operate as a professional learning community.

Learning by Doing

Since this is a book written for practitioners by practitioners, we want to do more than simply inform the reader about PRTI. This book is structured to lead you through a process not only to develop a deeper understanding of the relationship between POI and RTI, but also to create an actual pyramid response to intervention for your school. The end of each chapter poses essential questions that are linked to activities found in the appendix. Visit **go.solution-tree.com/rti** to download the activities and other helpful information. You and your team can use these to answer the following essential questions:

1. How do your school's current practices align with the essential elements of RTI?

2. How will your school respond to key RTI questions?

3. What elements of RTI are present in the pioneering models?

4. Have you created a foundation for your PRTI by implementing the essential characteristics of a professional learning community?

5. Who are your under-represented students?

6. What are all of your human and fiscal resources?

7. Are your current interventions aligned with the essential characteristics of Learning CPR?

8. What is your Tier 1 core program?

9. What are your Tier 2 supplemental interventions?

10. What are your Tier 3 intensive interventions?

11. What are your behavioral interventions?

12. How will you coordinate, document, and communicate about your PRTI?

13. Now that you have created a schoolwide, systematic PRTI, how will you begin implementation?

To begin the process, the next chapter discusses the main elements of response to intervention.

Chapter Two

The Facts About RTI

At first glance, response to intervention (RTI) is a method to identify learning disabilities. But, RTI could play a much larger role. It has the ability to transform how we educate students—all students. With RTI, students may get the support they need as soon as they show signs that they are having difficulty learning, regardless of whether or not they have a disability.

—Council for Exceptional Children

The student study team (SST) at Crabapple Elementary was stumped. Anna had transferred during the middle of kindergarten from Mexico; it was unclear whether she regularly attended school there. When she came to the United States, Anna spoke no English. First grade was a struggle for Anna, and some members of the SST have acknowledged that she did not have the best teacher. Anna failed to grasp phonics, her English was not developing, and she was falling farther and farther behind her peers.

The SST convened when Anna was halfway through first grade and recommended that she sit toward the front of the room, complete fewer homework problems each week, and attend after-school reading class twice a week for an hour. These interventions did not bring Anna's achievement to grade level, and at the end of the year, the SST recommended retention; Anna's parents and the principal (who had been members of the SST from the beginning) agreed.

Anna's second time through first grade has not met with more success. Although she has a better teacher, she's received the same interventions and does not seem to be retaining any knowledge from week to week or even day to day. In addition, Anna's behavior has begun to deteriorate. Although she generally is a sweet child, Anna now pesters others and avoids situations in which she is asked to read.

The SST knows that she automatically will be promoted to second grade because students are not retained twice at Crabapple, but they are out of ideas. The limited number of interventions they have employed has not had a sufficient effect. In addition, the team is unsure whether Anna qualifies for special education, and they haven't tried to identify her precise academic needs. Unless the SST requests special education assessment, Anna will fall further behind. But once in special education, Anna will probably never reach grade-level standards; she'll be stuck in special education forever.

Anna needs a solid core curriculum, a prompt diagnosis of her specific needs, and an academic prescription that targets her deficiencies with explicit, high-quality interventions. She needs a positive behavior contract that acknowledges and rewards her behavior and assignment completion. Instead, Anna's school has waited for her to fail before systemically assisting her. Now she needs mandatory, research-based supplements—taught by the best educators at Crabapple, frequently monitored for progress, and adjusted as needed. In short, Anna needs response to intervention (RTI), which holds great promise for students in situations like hers.

What Is RTI?

Response to intervention is the practice of 1) providing high-quality instruction and interventions that match students' needs and 2) using students' learning rate over time and level of performance to make important educational decisions.

High-quality instruction and interventions refers to the use of core instruction and interventions that have been demonstrated through scientific research to produce results in student learning. *Learning rate over time* means the growth in student achievement or behavior compared to the student's previous level of performance or to the growth of others in the same grade level or course of study. *Level of performance* refers to a student's progress compared to expected performance on either criterion-referenced or norm-referenced tests.

Educators base their decisions to apply interventions on information about the student's rate of learning over time and his or her level of performance. These decisions include, but are not limited to, providing more intense intervention in regular education and deciding whether a student should be placed in special education or exit from it.

RTI blends systematic and engaging assessment, instruction, and school-classroom-parent communication to relentlessly improve student learning. One byproduct may be reducing the number of children incorrectly identified with a learning disability. Interventions, which occur both before and after a referral to special education, are timely, diagnostic, intensive, systemic, and targeted.

In an RTI system, simply identifying a learning disability is not as important as collecting the observational data that will help determine the types of service the child needs. To make RTI work, psychologists, resource teachers, speech-language pathologists, reading specialists, and administrators need to become the kind of diagnosticians who can analyze a specific area of deficit *and* recommend the specific procedure or program that will address it. This requires specialized training, which is uncommon in most schools. It will also require that these educators consistently operate as a professional learning community, collaboratively focused on learning and results.

Some practitioners describe their RTI system as a problem-solving model (PSM; see chapter 3) and base their study of student needs on the scientific method (Education Evolving, 2005). For example, the state of Iowa has developed a PSM system that applies the following questions to each student situation (Education Evolving, 2005):

- What is the problem?
- Why does it exist?
- What should be done to address the problem?
- Did the intervention work? What comes next?

RTI involves all stakeholders in improving student learning. Among the organizations that recommend expanded roles for their members in developing and implementing RTI programs are the following:

- American Speech-Language-Hearing Association
- Division for Learning Disabilities of the Council for Exceptional Children
- International Dyslexia Association
- International Reading Association
- Learning Disabilities Association of America
- National Association of School Psychologists
- National Center for Learning Disabilities
- National Education Association
- School Social Work Association of America

Expanded roles for educators may mean providing in-class support, becoming involved in universal screening and progress monitoring, and participating actively in problem-solving in teams that monitor and analyze student success. By providing early, high-quality, and well-designed interventions to all students, and by using learning rate over time and levels of performance to monitor children's educational progress, these organizations and others hope to reduce the number of "curriculum casualties."

The Early History of RTI

The evolution of RTI dates from Stanley Deno's *cascade model,* developed in 1970. Deno's cascade model was historic because it envisioned a continuum of environments in which students with special needs could be served. It did so well before the passage of the Education for All Handicapped Children Act in 1975 (Public Law 94–142), which made it illegal to exclude students with disabilities from public schools and made serving students in the least restrictive environment the law of the land. Deno's cascade model outlined five progressively less restrictive environments in which to educate students with disabilities: home, special schools, self-contained classrooms, general education classrooms with pull-out support, and general education classrooms with full inclusion. The cascade model led to the inclusion movement to integrate students with special needs into regular education settings, where staff attempted, in some cases, to meet student needs *before* referring them for special education evaluation.

During the late 1980s and '90s, schools' efforts to apply the cascade approach were hamstrung by a lack of teacher readiness; general education teachers were inadequately trained to successfully teach students with special needs. Schools also hesitated to use the cascade approach for fear of violating student rights by delaying referral.

However, some aspects of the cascade model remain relevant. Part of Deno's work included developing *curriculum-based measures* (CBMs), precise, direct assessments of growth in students' academic skills that are short and straightforward enough to be administered frequently. Deno, Lynn Fuchs, and Phyllis Mirkin advocated using CBMs to measure student learning growth frequently and then to change instruction or even to raise student goals based on the results (Fuchs, Deno, & Mirkin, 1984). They eventually established rules to guide teachers in making these formative changes in instruction, intervention, and goals. CBMs still serve as appropriate progress-monitoring tools within an RTI system to determine the efficacy of instructional programs.

CBMs are standardized, reliable, valid, and brief (1–3 minute) assessments that include measurement tools, protocols, expected student growth rates, and periodic achievement benchmarks, measured through direct observation of students as they complete one-on-one assessments in the areas of reading, writing, and mathematics.

IDEA 1997 and IDEIA 2004

The cascade and inclusion models were probably intended to better serve the many students in special education; however, "they failed to utilize empirical evidence of effective practice and instead focused on philosophical issues about the moral imperative to educate all children" (Brown-Chidsey & Steege, 2005, p. x). In the traditional special education model, educators and student advocates have also focused on following procedural rules and regulations. In 1997, the Individuals with Disabilities Education Act (IDEA) urged educators to move beyond philosophical issues and compliance; IDEA emphasized a results-oriented system of special education over one in which implementation of the proper procedures alone was sufficient (Batsche et al., 2006).

Regulations must be followed, and when they are not, schools should be held accountable. IDEA recognized, however, that the academic *progress* that students make is equally important. In the traditional special education model, a student receives a research-based intervention, which may or may not be based on a specific need. In the new model of special education informed by the principles of RTI, mere implementation will not be sufficient. In the new model, the effect on student learning and the response of students in both general and special education to interventions are as important as following procedures.

Although IDEA 1997 introduced important new concepts and provisions, it resulted in little change in practice. The Individuals with Disabilities Education Improvement Act (IDEIA) of 2004 reauthorized IDEA and made a more forceful case for a results-oriented approach. IDEA 1997 allowed for 5% of Part B funds to be used for schoolwide early, prereferral interventions; IDEIA 2004 increases the percentage to 15%. (Part B funds outline services to children ages 3–21 who receive special education services.) Thus, although special education often encroaches on educational agencies' general funds, IDEIA 2004 supports assistance that begins early in a student's schooling and in general education settings. IDEA 1997 allowed students to qualify for special education based on their responses to intervention, a provision strengthened in IDEIA 2004. The following language clearly implies that no state should continue to use the discrepancy model:

> For these reasons, models that incorporate response to a research-based intervention should be given priority in any effort to identify students with SLD [specific learning disability]. Identification models that incorporate response to intervention represent a shift in special education toward the goals of better achievement and behavioral outcomes for students identified with SLD. (U.S. Department of Education, 2005, p. 35802)

Under IDEIA 2004, schools are no longer required to identify a severe discrepancy between academic achievement and intellectual ability to qualify a child with a specific learning disability for special education.

Why Now?

IDEIA's impact goes beyond special education, however. In trying to meet the needs of students at risk, we face the challenge of trying to bridge a real or perceived gap between general and special education. The current divided system of attempting to assist some students in general education and others in special education creates challenges. The type of academic interventions provided in the general classroom setting and in the pull-out special education classroom may be redundant, and conflicts result from educators' lack of coordination with each other, their focus on paperwork and legal process over results, and their assumption of separate spheres of responsibility for student learning.

In contrast, RTI provides a unified system of studying student difficulties and providing early intervention prior to referral for formal evaluation for special education or allowing such evaluation only as a last resort, as noted, for example, by Robert Wedl (Education Evolving, 2005). Such a system needs to be in place in all schools to serve Anna and students like her.

Current Relationship Between General and Special Education

- **Conflicts and redundancies**

- **Lack of coordination**

- **A focus on paperwork and legal processes over results**

- **Separate spheres of responsibility for students**

Today, sadly, students like Anna only receive assistance *after* they qualify for special education—that is, after a discrepancy is found between aptitude and achievement. The ultimate decision to qualify a child for special education should be made by a team of stakeholders only after high-quality interventions have been attempted and frequently monitored. Academic and psychological assessments can be used during the formal evaluation process to rule out the presence of low IQ or of attention, behavioral, or emotional problems; however, in an RTI system, the diagnostic investigation of a student's needs that would have most likely occurred during implementation may have already ruled out nonspecific learning disability factors. Nonetheless, the combination of information gathered in the RTI diagnosis and the formal evaluation process may help to very accurately identify students' specific needs (Education Evolving, 2005; Council for Exceptional Children, 2007).

Growing Support for RTI

Since 1999, at least four organizations—the National Institute of Child Health and Human Development's National Reading Panel, National Summit on Learning Disabilities (sponsored by the National Center for Learning Disabilities), the U.S. Department of Education's Office of Special Education Programs, and the President's Commission on Excellence in Special Education (the Commission)—have supported using RTI as an alternative to the discrepancy model by which most students traditionally qualify for special education. These organizations cite frequent misdiagnoses of students with special needs, a lack of early intervention, delays in delivering assistance, the infrequency with which students successfully exit special education, the use of inferior intervention programs, and other shortcomings in the traditional model of providing special assistance to students.

Educators have mistakenly (but with good intentions) placed too many students in special education. RTI promises to more accurately determine special education eligibility and may provide many more students with early, diagnostic, systematic, and explicit intervention.

Challenges Facing the Education of Students With Special Needs

- Misdiagnoses of student needs

- Lack of early intervention

- Delays in receiving assistance

- Infrequency of students exiting special education

- Use of inferior intervention programs

In fact, after analyzing the state of special education, the President's Commission on Excellence in Special Education (2002) concluded that although special education practices typically adhere to the law, they also tend to favor process over results. Special education is too often a destination instead of a system for providing supplementary supports. Moreover, for a student with a specific learning disability (SLD) to qualify for special education, the formal evaluation process requires a discrepancy between aptitude and achievement, as demonstrated by academic achievement that is below grade level—that is, failure.

Most schools do not emphasize prevention and early intervention, in part because they treat general and special education as separate entities, both instructionally and financially. The Commission also found that families have few options when special education services fail to make a difference and that the conflict and litigation that sometimes result divert staff resources and energies away from improving student learning.

Ultimately, then, educators' reliance on the discrepancy model may cause them to misdiagnose student needs and miss opportunities to assist students *before* they need special education services.

Finally, the Commission found that while the educators of children most at risk should be our most highly qualified, in fact, they often lack the requisite training and ongoing staff development to help maximize such students' learning. Too few research-based programs and systems are used, and there is a dearth of progress-monitoring instruments and models of data-informed adjustments to practice. Finally, schools tend to overemphasize compliance and bureaucratic requirements, but do not monitor students' academic and social achievement with enough care and regularity or adjust programs accordingly. The Commission recommended focusing on results over process (as in a professional learning community), on preventing failure rather than waiting for failure to qualify students for special education, and on general and special educators sharing responsibility for all children's maximal learning (President's Commission on Excellence in Special Education, 2002).

Response to intervention coincides with other promising educational developments. Since NCLB, there is an increased emphasis on using well-researched programs and improving core literacy curricula (per the Reading First program). In addition, school systems are increasingly considering systematic ways of providing assistance to students (such as

Recommendations of the President's
Commission on Excellence in Special
Education (2002)

- Focus on student results.

- Emphasize prevention.

- Use high-quality programs.

- Monitor progress and adjust instruction frequently.

- Share instructional and fiscal responsibility for student
  success between general and special education.

- Assign the most highly qualified staff
  to teach learners most at risk.

- Set high expectations for academic
  and social achievement.

through a pyramid of interventions, as part of becoming a professional learning community). NCLB accountability standards that require ever-increasing percentages of students to perform at grade level are also prompting a greater sense of urgency for accelerating student learning.

Moreover, schools have developed the use of formative assessments of students' learning (Stiggins, Arter, Chappuis, & Chappuis, 2004). Such assessments have included such universal screening and progress-monitoring tools as Dynamic Indicators of Basic Early Literacy Skills (DIBELS; Good & Kaminski, 2002) and other CBMs (Deno, 2003). Finally, schools have better met individual students' needs by increasing or improving differentiation of instruction (Tomlinson, 1999). All of these initiatives are important to improving student learning and are ideal complements to RTI.

Rejection of the Discrepancy Model

RTI developed in response to the shortcomings of the discrepancy model, which often waited for student educational failure before diagnosing a specific learning disability. Jack Fletcher and Carolyn Denton (2003) have shown that the discrepancy model can neither accurately identify student difficulties, which occur along a broad academic continuum, nor improve student learning; in fact, they argue, "the critical question is how such approaches lead to better outcomes for children with [learning disabilities]" (p. 5). Sally Shaywitz (2003) has shown that the reading difficulties of students in special education have at best stabilized as a result of traditional services; these students have not closed the gap toward grade-level proficiency. (Shaywitz favors systematic, research-based reading interventions based on students' specific diagnosed needs.)

To date, RTI has proven to be a more reliable way to identify which students require special education services. A team must take into account a student's native language and behavioral, socioeconomic, and educational background (collectively known as *environmental factors*) when determining whether a student qualifies for special education services; if there are environmental factors that may explain the poor academic performance, then IDEIA suggests that the student may not be eligible for special education. RTI is not subject to these environmental factors to the same extent, because in a well-designed RTI system, students who are considered for special education have already received systemic interventions and not shown progress—they have not responded to the interventions. Most importantly, a student's response to intervention informs all future efforts, helping ensure that the student succeeds.

These are some of the reasons educators should embrace RTI and embed it within the PLC structure. Of course, the most compelling reason to adopt RTI is that the Individuals with Disabilities Education Improvement Act (IDEIA) of 2004 endorses it (Public Law 108–446). RTI challenges the basic premises of some educators by assuming that *all* students can learn, that all educators will take responsibility for all learners, and that schools will adjust their current environments and practices so that this can occur. As Dave Tilly (2006) concludes, "RtI is likely the single best opportunity we have had to improve education for all students with disabilities—and students without them—that has occurred since the passage of the Education of the Handicapped Act in 1975" (p. 1).

A Systematic Response

RTI is not a program, but rather a system for meeting all students' needs. It is more of an evolution of existing organizational and educational practices than an educational revolution (Tilly III, 2006). RTI requires a more efficient use of resources, a research-based foundation, and a team approach to problem-solving on a student-by-student basis. The current system of general education, Title I education, education for English learners, and special education is not tiered, nor is it coherent and systematic. It is very rare for schools to provide systematic, schoolwide, and targeted interventions of any kind; different tiers of interventions are rarer still. While staff in general education, Title I, English learner, and special education programs are often working toward the same goal, they rarely communicate or collaborate. RTI promises to make general and special education stronger and more effective by using all the resources a school has to assist children. As Peter Senge (1990) suggests about organizational improvement, the *entire system* of meeting students' needs requires our attention; focusing on components piece by piece will not work.

Inevitably, schools that explore or implement RTI systems will need to reinterpret the roles of special and regular education staff (Bradley, Danielson, & Hallahan, 2002). Educators should proactively and clearly answer such questions as:

- At what stage or tier should special education staff begin intervening with students at risk?

- Who will oversee the process?

- Which interventions will take place in the regular classroom and which outside it?

- Who will undertake these interventions—regular classroom teachers, specialists, or special education teachers?

In an RTI system, interventions can and should be provided early— by regular and special education teachers, reading specialists, or qualified paraprofessionals, in small groups within the regular classroom or in separate reading or intervention rooms. RTI can help harness, systematically and coherently, the resources and expertise of specialists in general education, Title I education, English-language learner education, and special education.

An RTI system can provide earlier and perhaps superior intervention to students at risk, and it offers one other advantage over past practice: ongoing formal evaluation. As Renee Bradley, Louis Danielson, and Daniel Hallahan (2002) note, the data gathered from progress monitoring and frequent one-on-one or small-group meetings with children can allow more accurate diagnoses and specific program recommendations than the discrepancy model. This prereferral data allows educators to link evaluation to appropriate interventions, rather than use it simply to discover a discrepancy.

Moreover, frequent progress monitoring (brief probes of students' learning growth) under RTI continually informs adjustments to instruction. Using universal screening tools such as DIBELS, teachers can discover children's reading difficulties early on and respond to them before students have failed and their referral to special education is inevitable.

We need not and should not wait to assist students who are having learning problems. Consider that some 80% of students who receive special education experience reading difficulties (Shaywitz, 2003). This translates into approximately 4% of the total student population, which implies that at least one student in each primary grade class would benefit from early intervention. Early, diagnostic, explicit, and systematic interventions can help eliminate difficulties before they become entrenched (Shaywitz, 2003). The time is right and the time is now for RTI. While RTI research and regulations are relatively new, there are pioneering models that represent early efforts at more systematically meeting all students' needs. The next chapter describes several of these models.

How do your school's current practices align with the essential elements of RTI?

See page 172 for an activity to help you evaluate your school's practices in relation to RTI's essential elements. Discuss each of the essential elements, and honestly record your current reality. Next, record your long-term desired outcome, and establish a few short-term goals.

Visit **go.solution-tree.com/rti** to download this activity.

Chapter Three

RTI Models

We can't solve problems by using the same kind of thinking we used when we created them.

—Albert Einstein

Three months into the school year at Pine Elementary, a team of energetic fifth-grade teachers decided to screen all students with a benchmark reading comprehension assessment. Nearly 60% of the children scored remarkably low on questions testing their literal comprehension of passages. Many of these students had been working periodically with Pine's reading specialist, who arranged pull-out interventions in the area of literal comprehension.

Something was going wrong. But it was unclear whether the students who performed poorly needed more time and support to master literal comprehension, or whether they were casualties of a subpar curriculum. In a meeting with the fifth-grade team, the principal of Pine suggested, "If such a large percentage of students are failing, we have a major problem on our hands. We're going to need to look beyond just this class or grade level to find the root of the problem."

Two Systems of Implementation

As the principal at Pine realized, to meet the needs of all students, a school must have a coherent system of instruction and assessment to monitor student learning and respond systematically when data suggests problems exist. Pine doesn't need more pull-outs; it needs response to intervention.

RTI systems are characterized by 1) instruction and programs matched to student needs, often in tiers of instruction that differ in frequency and intensity, and 2) frequent progress monitoring to examine student progress and to inform teachers' adjustments to instructional plans. Higher tiers represent increasingly intensive interventions that address student needs. If a student fails to make progress despite increasingly intensive and targeted tiers of intervention, a referral to determine eligibility for special education may be necessary. Data gathered during diagnoses of student learning in these tiers of intervention will provide essential information to guide these formal evaluations. Researchers and practitioners acknowledge that RTI can take many forms, but the protocol system and the problem-solving system are the two primary forms.

The Protocol System

In the *protocol system*, students qualify for existing intervention programs according to pre-established criteria and the nature of the deficiency (such as fluency interventions for fluency deficiencies or comprehension interventions for comprehension deficiencies). Specialists train intervention staffs on one program per area. In literacy, for example, the school would use one program schoolwide for reading comprehension, instead of different comprehension interventions for slightly different diagnosed needs. In the protocol model, teacher training and supervision to ensure program implementation with fidelity are simpler, team meetings to discuss student plans are more efficient, and evaluation, progress monitoring, and validation of program efficacy are more straightforward (McCook, 2006).

The Problem-Solving System

The *problem-solving system* utilizes staff members' input to identify highly individualized student plans. Because team members consider more learning options, they can prescribe a more specific learning plan for each student and select students on less strict *cut points* than in the protocol model. For example, if the cut point in the protocol model is the ability to read 20 words per minute by the middle of first grade, any student who lacked that ability would automatically receive a predetermined intervention. In the problem-solving model, however, students slightly below and above the cut point are diagnosed individually. Some may need a broader phonological support, others may need a more narrow phonetic support, and still others may simply receive slightly more targeted and individualized attention from the classroom teacher. Under the problem-solving model, staff may be more likely to embrace the selected intervention because their expertise has been used to make diagnostic decisions. As the student study team (SST) considers more programs for unique student needs, this model requires more teacher training on a diverse set of programs, which are then more difficult to monitor. Principals and reading specialists may have to spend more time ensuring that the intervention staff implements programs uniformly.

Protocol System	*Problem-Solving System*
• Pre-established qualification criteria	• More specific student plans, created with more staff input
• Limited number of intervention programs	• Multiple intervention programs
• Straightforward staff training, progress monitoring, and decision-making	• More complex training, progress monitoring, and decision-making

Many RTI manuals recommend a blended program that incorporates the best of both the protocol and problem-solving systems. It is critical that the SST obtain external validations of student progress and continue to diagnose problems during the intervention, so that the team can make well-thought-out adjustments to student learning plans. Problem-solving teams may want to persist in searching for solutions to a particular learning problem, but they also should help students move through increasingly intensive tiers of assistance, including evaluation for a learning disability, if necessary (McCook, 2006). Like many problem-solving models, blended models include a cycle of inquiry that involves defining student needs, developing a plan, implementing it, and evaluating the plan.

Regardless of the complexity of programs and levels of intensity in differing RTI models, Lynn Fuchs and Doug Fuchs note that RTI "integrate[s] increasingly intensive instruction and, at each layer, employ[s] assessment to identify students who are inadequately responsive and who therefore require intervention at the next, more intensive layer in the system" (2006, p. 621).

> In addition to tiered academic interventions, RTI includes a tiered system of identifying and providing behavioral interventions. Educators long have utilized the tiered models of effective behavior systems and positive behavior systems to describe the different types of student behaviors a school may encounter and to provide a framework for providing differentiated assistance (Sugai & Horner, 2006).

Documenting student progress and communicating with all stakeholders, particularly parents, are crucial. Again, RTI is not meant to supplant special education; rather, it tries to make the system of helping all students achieve more effective by intervening early and by diagnosing their specific needs more accurately.

Implementing and Monitoring an RTI System

RTI systems differ in terms of who is responsible for implementing interventions at each tier and in the nature and number of steps researchers recommend for implementation, from 4 (Fuchs & Fuchs, 2005) to 10

(McCook, 2006). Typically, steps increase in intensity as student needs become greater or when students fail to respond to less intensive interventions (Fuchs & Fuchs, 2005, 2007; McCook, 2006; Brown-Chidsey & Steege, 2005; Burdette, 2007). These steps include:

- Implementing a core program (Tier 1)

- Employing universal screening

- Implementing a classroom intervention

- Monitoring students' progress in the core program

- Initiating a supplemental (Tier 2) intervention

- Monitoring student progress to the supplemental intervention

- Initiating an intensive (Tier 3) intervention

- Monitoring student progress in response
  to the intensive intervention

- Assessing students to determine whether
  they have a learning disability

RTI systems hope that most students will respond to the core program at Tier 1, the supplemental interventions at Tier 2, or intensive interventions at Tier 3 before formal evaluation to determine special education eligibility becomes necessary. When a student's response to all interventions proves dramatically inferior to that of peers, he or she may have a learning disability. In that case, informed by the data collected during tiered interventions, teams find it easier to determine the nature of a child's learning disability and to design the personalized interventions that he or she requires.

Each "dose" of tiered support should last 6 to 8 weeks. Supplemental Tier 2 interventions occur at least 3 days a week for 30 minutes a session, in groups of three to six students. Sessions involve programs that are researched-based, explicit, systematic, and specific to student needs. Intensive Tier 3 interventions occur daily for 30 minutes in smaller groups. Interventions conducted after a student has qualified for special education involve truly individualized instruction and assistance, using the most specific and detailed programs, delivered by the most expert teachers. The amount of time and the level of support are constantly adjusted to ensure the level of learning remains high for all children (DuFour & Eaker, 1998).

At all tiers, interventions are typically supplementary in nature; they are not meant to replace the core program, but to provide additional, more targeted exposure to core concepts. However, some RTI models *do* supplant the core program with more basic, comprehensive interventions for students who are several grade levels behind (particularly in fourth grade or above) (B. Tollestrup, personal communication, June 5, 2007). For example, the California Department of Education (2002) has identified five reading intervention programs for students who are two or more grade levels behind.

Steps in RTI Systems

- A solid core program (Tier 1)
- Universal screening
- Differentiated support within the Tier 1 program
- Progress monitoring of students within the core program
- Supplemental (Tier 2) interventions to students slightly below grade level
- Progress monitoring of students within a supplemental intervention
- Intensive interventions (Tier 3) to students well below grade level
- Progress monitoring of students within an intensive intervention
- Referral for formal evaluation for special education eligibility

As states, districts, and schools design RTI systems, Fuchs and Fuchs (2007) suggest that their success will be at least partially based on their answers to six questions:

1. How many tiers of intervention will the school provide?

2. How will the school identify students who need intervention?

3. Will the school employ more of a problem-solving or a protocol approach?

4. What is an adequate response to intervention?

5. What does formal special education evaluation look like?

6. What is the function of special education in the context of the entire system?

While RTI is meant to meet students' needs before special education is required, it also impacts special education. If, after lack of response to high-quality interventions, a student is referred to special education, then that most intensive of interventions must become more individualized, while also utilizing the same solid instructional, programmatic, and progress-monitoring principles found in earlier RTI tiers.

Fuchs and Fuchs (2007) pose the following criteria to determine whether a student has responded adequately to an intervention:

- Is the student's performance at the end of the intervention above the 24th percentile— that is, within the normal range?

- Is his or her performance considered at grade level as defined by a criterion-based assessment?

- Is the student's slope of improvement adequate in comparison to peers, and is he or she on track to achieve grade-level proficiency?

- Has the student responded to intervention?

Educators should base their answers to the last question on a student's inadequate slope of progress and final level of performance at the end of the intervention.

RTI in Pioneering Schools

Schools, districts, consortiums, and states have designed and implemented RTI-like systems since the early 1990s. In this section, we describe the systems in a school and school district in southern California, a school district in northern California, a consortium of school districts in Iowa, and Washington state. Their approaches differ in specific strategies. Some *pull* students out of class to a classroom in which students from across the school receive supplementary intervention instruction. Others *push* extra teachers or paraprofessionals into general education classrooms, where they provide supplementary intervention instruction to small flexible groups. However, the goals of the programs are the same: to provide students with the early, targeted intervention support they need to progress to grade-level goals; to prevent them from developing more severe difficulties; and to reduce the number of unnecessary referrals to special education.

TLC

A large suburban school district south of Los Angeles has developed an approach to RTI known as Teaming for the Learning of all Children (TLC) (P. Watkins, personal communication, May 31, 2007). In TLC schools, staff universally screen students, using both standardized multiple-response examinations and other CBM-like assessments. TLC schools utilize four additional special education staff members (two certificated, two paraprofessional) to help meet student needs in reading and mathematics, regardless of the student's special education status.

TLC educators try to serve the needs of students with individualized education plans (IEPs) within regular classroom settings. In each grade, students with similar needs are distributed among regular education teachers and special education staff. Expert, highly trained educators teach students at risk in small groups of four to six.

The content and concepts students study in a given grade level and subject area are the same as in the core curriculum, but instruction, pedagogic approach, and pacing are adjusted to meet their specific needs. Children with diagnosed needs in areas of literacy such as phonemic awareness, fluency, or comprehension also receive assistance with research-based supplementary programs. Instructors meet unique student needs via differentiated small groups. In addition, regular classroom teachers often offer students a second, and even third, iteration of core reading and math instruction during leveled instructional time.

TLC operates on the principles of a professional learning community; it is a problem-solving model, in which the TLC team communicates student needs and successes to regular education staff during weekly release time.

Under TLC, students move fluidly between leveled groups. The school's leadership team, comprised of grade-level lead teachers and TLC staff, makes all important decisions concerning such movements. While educators engage in progress monitoring as recommended by most RTI models, the lines between tiers are blurred. Students receive differentiated and supplementary instruction daily, and do not necessarily move from Tier 1 to Tier 2 to Tier 3 intervention. When intervention is required, students receive every type of targeted intervention that the school possesses and deems necessary.

Groups differ in terms of size and students' abilities. General education classroom teachers, with additional TLC team members in the same classroom, provide reading instruction simultaneously to all students in a given grade level. Because the entire TLC staff teaches all students at a grade level en masse, administrators must schedule reading blocks at distinct times of the day for each grade level. Therefore, first graders might have a reading block the first hour of the school day, second graders during the second hour, and fifth graders during the last hour.

A goal of TLC, which resembles inclusion models from the 1990s, is to reduce referrals to special education. TLC requires a reallocation of resources and, more importantly, a paradigm shift for teachers. Teachers must become accustomed to collaborating and truly taking responsibility for the learning of all the students in their classroom, regardless of readiness or abilities, as well as for all the other students in their grade level and in the entire school.

For TLC administrators, a particular challenge is how to schedule both teachers and students so that small group and differentiated instruction can take place. Administrators must determine the amount of initial and ongoing staff development that teachers need, and the amount of time they require to give assessments to students and to share their results with colleagues.

The beliefs that govern TLC are consistent with those that inspire PLCs and RTI systems:

- Students receive instruction based on their individual needs.

- TLC staff members design individualized learning plans for students at risk that outline the core and supplementary instruction that they will receive from highly trained professionals.

- Learners at risk, including students with IEPs, receive supplementary services within the regular education setting.

- Teams provide assistance to special learners in small groups whenever possible.

- The neediest students learn in classrooms with the lowest student-teacher ratios during leveled instructional times.

In some school districts, students with disabilities and other unique needs often must travel to other schools in the same district for specialized instruction. For example, students with autistic or emotional disturbance diagnoses may be collectively instructed at a few sites across a local educational agency or region. Like full-inclusion models, TLC schools reject this model and instead attempt to meet all student needs through differentiated instruction in regular education settings at their home schools.

Early intervention and preventative supports are central to TLC schools. Students need not qualify for special education to receive assistance; those who have academic deficits and those who display gifted characteristics *all* receive differentiated instruction. Due to this early intervention, TLC educators may refer fewer students to special education, even students who have been previously diagnosed with a learning disability by other schools.

ExCEL

TLC was based in part on the ExCEL (Excellence: A Commitment to Every Learner) model from a high desert school district in southern California just northeast of Los Angeles. ExCEL attempts to assist all students, whether they are high achieving, struggling, or in between. The district's educators had discovered that their schools were not providing enough enrichment to their highest achieving students because most teaching targeted average or below-average students, and student learning followed these expectations.

The program's executive director notes that ExCEL, while based on an RTI model, has some distinctive characteristics (C. Bergen, personal communication, June 4, 2007). ExCEL views student movement through tiers or stages in a fluid continuum; changes in the intensity and nature of supports are frequent. The system's first priority, as with both the POI and

RTI, is universal access to a high-quality core program for all students. The second tier involves small groups that are leveled according to student ability; ExCEL educators do whatever it takes to help students within this tier learn.

Under ExCEL, student movement between leveled groups is fluid, progress monitoring is frequent, expectations for all students are high, and no additional expenditures are required. The district has experienced a reduction in the number of students in special education; students who now qualify for such services truly have significant disabilities. In addition, poor or inadequate instruction is eliminated as an explanation for failure to achieve grade-level goals.

ExCEL's system of early intervention, prevention of future problems, and acceleration won many accolades in its first 10 years, including the 2005 *American School Board Journal's* Magna Award. (Magna Awards annually recognize school districts for outstanding programs that advance student learning and encourage community involvement). Educators in the district now conduct ExCEL training across the state and the country.

CAST

ExCEL was derived from Neverstreaming, a play on the word *mainstreaming*—the practice of including special education students in general education settings. CAST (Collaborative Academic Support Teams) is also derived from Neverstreaming, but has qualities that make it distinct from ExCEL and TLC, as noted by the director of special education responsible for Neverstreaming and CAST in a large northern California district near Sacramento, one of the first in the nation to embrace RTI-like concepts (B. Tollestrup, personal communication, June 5, 2007). For example, interventions, which are available for all students, are the responsibility of the general education staff; special education teachers are not responsible for remediating students at risk.

In the first years after initiating the Neverstreaming model in 1992, the district annually referred roughly 1,800 of its 30,000 students for special education testing. By 2005, the number of annual special education referrals had been cut in half, even though the district enrollment had doubled. The district changed the name from Neverstreaming to CAST to remove the special education connotation; CAST educators view all students, including those who receive special education services, as general education students first and foremost.

Within the CAST program, a team comprised of the site administrator, resource teacher, psychologist, reading specialist, and speech pathologist problem-solves with classroom teachers, who bring student concerns to the group's attention. In quarterly follow-up meetings, the team examines each student's learning trajectory.

Regular classroom teachers provide interventions to small groups of students who have learning gaps that can be ameliorated by supplementing the core literacy program. Specialists periodically support the classroom teacher in delivering targeted interventions (for example, in decoding or fluency). Students who are far below grade level and who fail to respond to Tier 2 within-the-classroom interventions receive Tier 3 intensive instruction that supplants their core literacy program. These students' severe needs involve deficiencies in basic skills and knowledge that cannot be met by differentiating or supplementing the core program.

Students have responded. The district has found that most children who initially experience difficulties are not learning disabled, but instead are "curriculum casualties": Educators had overlooked or underserved them. When this district's type of RTI began many years ago, its students were scoring in the 20th percentile in reading; by 2007 in a larger, more diverse district, they were in the 60th percentile.

The HAEA Model

The systematic RTI efforts of the Heartland Area Education Agency (HAEA), a large consortium of school districts in Iowa that serves one fourth of the state's public education students, have benefitted over 130,000 students annually.

In the late 1980s, the HAEA realized that although it was implementing special education programs as well as possible, the entire *system* had to get better. General education teachers were differentiating and individualizing instruction as much as they could without the support of additional staff, and special education staff were following rules and regulations. Yet students were still being referred for formal evaluation to special education at increasing rates, and once in special education, students were not progressing to grade-level proficiency or returning to general education.

So the consortium decided to develop a system that more systemically provided targeted academic support to students. They implemented a problem-solving model in which teachers identified and referred children who needed additional assistance on a case-by-case, student-by-student basis. Teachers who were trained in special education supported general education classroom teachers in providing increasingly intensive interventions. The consortium overcame early obstacles to collaboration (for example, general education teachers were not particularly interested in input from special education colleagues). They also concluded, through observation and feedback, that general education teachers could successfully provide systematic intervention services to only one or two students at a time.

The HAEA realized that its staff needed to make the process of identifying students and providing needed support to them more efficient. According to the HAEA's director, the existing system's "science" was right, but its "engineering" needed help (D. Tilly, personal communication, December 11, 2007). The schools were not adequately serving students with similar challenges. When they discerned the number and nature of student difficulties, HAEA administrators elected to implement group-level interventions. With the introduction of Reading First at the federal and local levels to provide grants to schools and school systems that progressively ameliorated students' reading deficiencies, the HAEA system transformed itself by introducing a pyramid of interventions.

Today, HAEA educators address student gaps through the use of specific diagnostic instruments that assess deficiencies and prescribe a specific course of study. For example, in the area of reading comprehension, educators employ Curriculum-Based Evaluation (developed by Kenneth Howell, Sheila Fox, and Mada Kay Morehead at Western Washington University) to analyze a hierarchy of potential student deficiencies until they find the probable cause of a child's difficulty. The system of interventions in HAEA contains the key elements of RTI: diagnose, prescribe, measure, monitor, and adjust. Educators provide students whose limited progress reveals that they need different or additional support with interventions of increasing intensity, frequency, and duration.

Parents continue to request formal evaluations of their children. When formal evaluation to determine eligibility for special education is requested, the student's response to the previous interventions provides a key piece of data. Parents also are key members of the problem-solving team, and educators constantly inform them about the interventions their children are receiving.

After reviewing a body of evidence on a student, an HAEA team bases its decisions regarding the student's placement in special education using these criteria:

- The student has not responded to interventions at an acceptable rate, or the level of assistance that he or she needs is too great to continue without special education services.

- Even with additional supports, a significant discrepancy exists between the student's performance and that of peers or grade-level standards.

- The student has instructional needs that cannot be met in a supplemented general education environment; the team of educators has identified a different educational environment that will meet the child's needs.

The system is reluctant to remove students from the core curriculum and instead prefers to provide them with *supplemental* supports. A team decides which portions of the core curriculum are relevant and can be successfully accessed by the students. For example, HAEA staff do not pull students from reading to give them reading interventions. Students who experience difficulties in reading still continue to receive core instruction in reading, as well as supplemental interventions in their specifically diagnosed areas of need.

In general, HAEA educators believe that NCLB requires them to use scientifically based curricula and practices; they view RTI as their delivery model for doing so.

The Washington Model

Several states also have implemented systematic initiatives for students at risk. Washington, for example, has prepared RTI-related resources and supports for all schools. Washington stresses that it is providing a system for all students; its superintendent of education in particular has emphasized personalized education, data-based decision-making, universal screening, collaboration, progress monitoring, and continuous evaluation and improvement of programs and instruction (Washington

State Department of Education, 2006). While RTI systems in Washington vary from district to district, they share seven core principles:

1. Use all school resources to help all students learn.

2. Use research-based programs and instruction.

3. Focus on the core program.

4. Universally screen students so that none fall through the cracks.

5. Use a multitiered approach to meeting student needs.

6. Use data to drive decision-making.

7. Monitor progress often. (Washington State Board of Education, 2006)

TLC: A team of specialists works with students at every grade level throughout the day to provide differentiated reading intervention to small groups.

ExCEL: Specialists provide students small group supplementary intervention when frequently given assessments reveal a need.

CAST: Classroom teachers and specialists provide small group support within the general education classroom; students significantly below grade-level standards receive a new core curriculum that supplants the existing one.

HAEA: General and special educators work together to diagnose student needs, prescribe interventions, measure and monitor student progress, and adjust individualized student plans as needed.

Washington: The state sets expectations for schools and school districts to implement RTI systems for helping all students learn.

These schools, school districts, consortiums, and states have made a commitment to reform "business as usual." Each organization tries to provide students with targeted interventions as soon as their needs are diagnosed, so as to reduce unnecessary referrals to special education and ensure that all students receive what they need to achieve grade-level proficiency.

A New Way of Educating All Children

These models represent a few of the early, successful ways in which schools and school districts have implemented components of RTI in their efforts to serve all children well. We are certain many other examples exist.

The point is that RTI represents a new way of educating *all* children. In this new model, students receive access to a high-quality core curriculum, with differentiation and scaffolding. Teachers frequently administer a universal screening instrument and analyze results to assess student learning and the quality of the core program. Tiers of intervention with increasing levels of intensity and specificity provide support to students who do not respond to their current level of instruction. Following their diagnoses of student needs, a team chooses research-based, systematic interventions, which highly trained educators then deliver.

Elements of Response to Intervention in a Professional Learning Community

- Collective responsibility by all staff for all students

- Access to a high-quality core curriculum

- True differentiation in the classroom

- Universal screening

- Analyses of student work to evaluate overall curriculum and diagnose individual student needs

- Tiers of intervention

- Systematic, explicit, and research-based programs, diagnostically chosen and taught by the most effective educators

Educators use core and intervention programs with fidelity. They engage in continuous progress monitoring for students in more intensive tiers. They respect student and parent rights as outlined in IDEIA 2004 regulations regarding a free appropriate public education in the least restrictive environment, and make referrals to special education evaluation only when truly appropriate. Imagine that Anna, the struggling second grader described in the beginning of chapter 2, were a student in an RTI school. She probably would not become a curriculum casualty who had already been retained, with no hope but special education. Similarly, if Pine Elementary were implementing RTI, 60% of the students would never be allowed to fail.

In an RTI system, services are available to all students, including those receiving services under Title I, Title III, or IDEIA. While schools cannot spend the 15% of IDEIA Part B funds dedicated to early intervening services (EIS) on students already identified under IDEIA—EIS funds can only be spent on students not already in special education—this does not preclude schools from providing RTI interventions to students in special education using funding from other sources. All students in need should receive assistance, regardless of the funding source or the educator with whom they work.

A Unified Approach

A critical lesson from RTI is that general and special education must not be considered as separate programs. In one elementary school in north San Diego County, the special education resource teacher meets with special education students during the period before lunch. During the period after lunch, she teaches small group classes comprised of some children who receive special education services and some who do not. Based on their needs, all students attend support classes taught by a variety of highly trained teachers; in addition, students in special education receive other services as prescribed by their individualized education plans (IEPs). For example, if a student's diagnosed areas of need include expressive and receptive language deficiencies, a speech and language pathologist offers him or her intervention services several times a week. If a student's IEP includes written language goals, the student might receive 30 minutes of daily support to write a paragraph independently. The critical point is that all staff serve all students based on their needs—even those who do not have an IEP.

In this new system, special education staff serve regular education students, and special education students receive interventions from regular education staff. Students receive direct services as identified in their IEPs as well as other assistance the school can bring to bear. For example, a student with receptive and expressive language needs and written language goals may be slightly below grade level in fluency. While his fluency needs may not be significant enough to be addressed in his IEP, this student will receive daily targeted fluency intervention together with all other children whose fluency is also slightly below grade level. The student would receive the services outlined in his IEP during the first few hours of the day, and later would receive fluency assistance during the last half hour of the day.

RTI both diagnoses specific student needs and prescribes specific interventions. The nature and degree of those needs may place some students in a supplementary (Tier 2) intervention; other students, whose deficiencies place them well below grade level, may need to receive an intensive (Tier 3) intervention. We do not recommend that schools first assign a student to a tier and then offer academic supports and interventions based on that tier. Rather, we suggest that staff first diagnose needs and then provide the supports needed to meet them. The process may suggest a certain tier, but a rigid interpretation of whether a student "belongs" in Tier 2 or Tier 3 should not drive the interventions the student receives; only the student's needs should do so.

RTI is still evolving, and schools will still necessarily be influenced and guided by regulations originating at the local, state, and federal level, including IDEIA 2004. We hope that the suggestions in the following chapters will aid schools in meeting the regulations' requirements. For particular questions you may have, please consult state regulations and the directives of local educational agencies.

How will your school respond to key RTI questions?

See page 173 for an activity to help your leadership team evaluate your school's practices in relation to RTI's key questions. Discuss and answer each of the key questions, and honestly record your current reality. Next, record your long-term desired outcome, and establish a few short-term goals.

*What elements of RTI are present
in the pioneering models?*

See page 174 for an activity to monitor the progress of your leadership team's knowledge of RTI. Review each of the early RTI models described in chapter 3, and identify the evidence that these models have included the key components of RTI.

Visit **go.solution-tree.com/rti**
to download these activities.

Chapter Four

Laying the Foundation: A Professional Learning Community

We embrace explicitly the proposition that effective practice and popular practice are very likely two different things.

**—Douglas Reeves, chairman and founder,
The Leadership and Learning Center**

*E*lm Elementary School is located in a suburban area of moderate socioeconomic status on the Eastern seaboard. It's not the poorest elementary school in the district, but its students consistently score below the state average, and parents regularly request to transfer their children to other schools. In theory, Elm's student study team (SST) provides a systematic, schoolwide intervention process, yet teachers rarely refer children. Instead, most teachers want to "keep" their kids, choosing to handle all student needs on their own. The few teachers who do regularly make referrals have tried limited in-class interventions and offer few helpful observations or hard data on student performance to inform the student study team.

One or two teachers who refer students to the team have tried everything they know, but unfortunately, their efforts have not made a significant difference in student learning. Given Elm's below-average scores in state assessments, the district office has directed the school leadership team to develop and implement a more effective intervention program to support students at risk. At their first meeting, however, the team sat in silence. No one knew where to begin.

Reculturing Your School

As the previous two chapters have clearly demonstrated, RTI is not merely a new process to identify students with special needs, nor should it be viewed as primarily a special education initiative or a supplemental intervention program. Instead, RTI is a schoolwide, systematic, collaborative process in which all school resources are seamlessly integrated and singularly focused on the same outcome—to ensure that every student learns at high levels. As the leadership team at Elm Elementary discovered, achieving this outcome demands much more than creating a student study team or identifying supplemental interventions. To successfully implement RTI, a staff must dissolve the cultural and structural barriers between regular education and special education to create a collective response in which core instruction and supplemental support form a learning continuum to meet the individual needs of every student.

Because this expectation of collective responsibility for learning is a radical departure from the way most schools have functioned for the past 4 decades, implementing RTI will take both a restructuring of school procedures *and* a reculturing of a staff's fundamental assumptions and beliefs. Considering that many schools have developed a strong resistance to change, how does a staff create the conditions necessary to ensure that all students learn?

Fortunately, there has never been greater consensus on what schools must do to achieve this ambitious goal. In 1998, Richard DuFour and Robert Eaker published *Professional Learning Communities at Work: Best Practices for Enhancing Student Achievement*, which provided the conceptual framework and supporting research for professional learning communities (PLCs). Subsequently, nearly all the leading educational organizations in North America endorsed PLCs as best practice, including, among others:

- The National Commission on Teaching and America's Future

- The National Education Association

- The National Association of Elementary School Principals

- The National Association of Secondary School Principals

- The National Staff Development Council

In 2005, many of North America's most respected educational researchers contributed to *On Common Ground* (DuFour, Eaker, & DuFour, 2005c), in which they demonstrated how their research validated and complemented essential PLC practices. Contributors included Roland Barth, Michael Fullan, Lawrence Lezotte, Douglas Reeves, Jonathon Saphier, Mike Schmoker, Dennis Sparks, and Rick Stiggins.

Finally, numerous PLC schools across North America are closing achievement gaps and achieving exceptional student achievement results, as documented at www.allthingsplc.info. With such overwhelming evidence and professional consensus on the effectiveness of PLCs, it is unconscionable for educators to disregard these facts and continue to implement ineffective, outdated teaching practices. Such actions are literally educational malpractice.

The essential characteristics of a professional learning community are perfectly aligned with the fundamental elements of response to intervention. Quite simply, PLC and RTI are complementary processes, built upon a proven research base of best practices and designed to produce the same outcome—high levels of student learning. PLCs create the schoolwide cultural and structural foundation necessary to implement a highly effective RTI program. Pyramid response to intervention, PRTI, forges PLC and RTI practices into a single powerful process to improve student learning. The first step in creating a PRTI is to implement the three "big ideas" of being a PLC: a focus on learning, a collaborative culture, and a focus on results.

A Focus on Learning

A PLC school's core mission is not simply to ensure that all students are *taught*, but also that they *learn*. As Richard DuFour, Rebecca DuFour,

Robert Eaker, and Thomas Many (2006) state in *Learning by Doing*:

> The very essence of a learning community is a focus on and a commitment to the learning of each student. When a school or district functions as a PLC, educators within the organization embrace high levels of learning for all students as both the reason the organization exists and the fundamental responsibility of those who work within it. (p. 3)

This seismic shift from a focus on teaching to a focus on learning is far more than a school slogan or a catchy "Learning for All" motto on its letterhead. Two fundamental assumptions underlie the mission of high levels of learning for all students: 1) Educators believe that all students are capable of high levels of learning, and 2) they accept responsibility for making this outcome a reality for every child.

Unfortunately, most schools embrace an entirely opposite outlook and hold fast to the belief that the socioeconomic factors of poverty, race, and language ultimately determine student success. If a majority of the school staff does not believe that they or their students have the ability to overcome these outside factors, what is the likelihood that they will succeed? All too often, a school's cultural beliefs become a self-fulfilling prophecy.

While some teachers may initially feel that they face insurmountable obstacles, the facts about student potential paint an entirely different picture. The Effective Schools research of Ron Edmonds, Larry Lezotte, Wilbur Brookover, Michael Rutter, and others proved conclusively that all children can learn and that schools control the factors to assure that students master core curriculum. In *What Works in Schools*, Robert Marzano (2003) notes that "an analysis of research conducted over a thirty-five year period demonstrates that the schools that are highly effective produce results that almost entirely overcome the effects of student backgrounds" (p. 7). Doug Reeves (2001) documented the success of 90/90/90 schools— schools in which at least 90% of students are eligible for free or reduced price lunch, at least 90% are from ethnic minorities, and at least 90% meet grade-level academic standards.

With such irrefutable evidence, a school that honestly tries to answer these three critical questions must conclude that the issue is not *whether* all students can learn at high levels, but rather *what* the school must do to secure the same results for their students. By creating a schoolwide focus on learning, a school simultaneously will be creating a culture of collective responsibility—an essential characteristic of RTI implementation. In the end, Larry Lezotte (2005) summed it up best: "Our experience verifies that the possibilities are unlimited once a dedicated school staff goes in search of research and best practices to advance their shared vision of learning for all. However, until they embrace the possibility that all children can learn, the obstacles and barriers they will find are virtually endless and will seem insurmountable" (p. 74).

A Collaborative Culture

Because no teacher can possibly possess all the knowledge, skills, time, and resources needed to ensure high levels of learning for all his or her students, educators at a PLC school work in collaborative teams. Collaboration does not happen by invitation or chance; instead, frequent team time is embedded into the teachers' contracted day. This allows disciplinary teams to work interdependently to achieve common goals linked to their collective mission of learning for all. PLC collaboration involves more than collegiality; it digs deeply into learning. PLC educators engage in disciplined inquiry and continuous improvement to "raise the bar" and "close the gap" of student learning and achievement (Fullan, 2005, p. 209). To this end, team efforts start by focusing on the first critical question of a professional learning community: "What is it we expect students to learn?"

To create an effective PRTI, teachers of the same course or grade level must first collectively determine what they expect all their students to know and be able to do. After all, a PRTI team cannot possibly create a systematic, collective response when students do not learn if individual teachers focus on different essential learning standards. Additionally, teacher teams must be empowered to select the essential learning outcomes, rather than these being determined solely by local, state, or national mandates. By identifying essential or "power" standards, teams can analyze, prioritize, and otherwise unpack the standards that describe what is most essential for students to know. Professional learning communities add value to standards by analyzing, synthesizing, and prioritizing them in a way that allows every teacher to allocate time and instructional focus toward a common goal. Only when a school has undertaken this process can it proceed to the next component of excellence: assessment for learning (Reeves, 2005).

A Focus on Results

After identifying the knowledge and skills that all students must learn, collaborative teams focus on the second critical question of a PLC: "How will we know if our students are learning?" Educators at a PLC school must assess their efforts to achieve high levels of learning for all students based on concrete results rather than good intentions. Just as IDEIA (2004) pushes educators to think beyond regulatory compliance to examine outcomes for students, a PLC pushes us to think beyond teaching to examine learning. This focus leads each collaborative team to create a series of common formative assessments to measure each student's progress toward mastery of essential learning outcomes (DuFour et al., 2006). Student assessment information constitutes the "life blood" of a PRTI; it is used to identify students in need of additional time and support and to confirm which core instructional strategies are most effective in meeting students' needs. Without timely assessment information, a school's intervention program assumes a "buckshot" approach, with teachers randomly "firing" broad intervention efforts and hoping that they "hit" a few students. Frequent, formative common assessments also provide the foundation for the progress monitoring needed to properly implement response to intervention.

Finally, because PLCs focus on results, they strive for continuous improvement through action experimentation: "Members of a professional learning community are action-oriented: They move quickly to turn aspirations into action and visions into reality" (DuFour et al., 2006, p. 4). All collaborative learning, planning, and goal-setting are useless until put into action. Unless staff members are willing to try new things, improvement in student learning is impossible. PLC educators do not view experimentation as a singular task to be accomplished; rather, they embrace experimentation as "how we do things" every day. Human nature tends to view change as an uncomfortable process, but in a PLC, the team should feel uneasy *without* change, for without change, there is no opportunity for improvement. Action experimentation is perfectly aligned with response to intervention; the central concept behind RTI, after all, is to apply research-based interventions for a struggling student, then measure the "learning" response to the intervention.

Additionally, this action orientation provides adult learning opportunities, as there is no better way to learn than by doing. Roland Barth says, "Ultimately there are two kinds of schools: learning enriched schools and learning impoverished schools. I have yet to see a school where the learning curves . . . of the adults were steep upward and those of the students were not. Teachers and students go hand and hand as learners . . . or they don't go at all" (2001, p. 23). When making critical decisions about teaching and learning, PLC teams engage in *collective inquiry* to continually learn about best practices. Teams do not make decisions merely by sharing experiences or averaging opinions, but instead by building shared knowledge through learning together. This collaborative learning enables team members to develop new skills to better meet the learning needs of their students. By building shared knowledge of best instructional practices, each team is now prepared to best meet the RTI requirements of implementing quality interventions with fidelity and efficacy.

When comparing the essential characteristics of being a PLC and the fundamental elements of RTI, one can see that these two powerful processes are not merely similar, but perfectly aligned to support the same outcomes.

For schools that have already started down the road to being to PLC, implementing RTI will not be a new initiative, but instead a validation and a deepening of their current practices. For schools like Elm Elementary that have not started down this road, RTI will seem like a nearly impossible undertaking. Trying to implement RTI without first creating a school culture and structure aligned with PLC practices would be like trying to

PLC Essential Characteristics		RTI Fundamental Elements
Focus on Learning & Collaborative Culture	⟶	Collective Responsibility
Focus on Results	⟶	Universal Screening & Progress Monitoring
Action Experimentation	⟶	Systematic Interventions & Decision Protocols
Collective Inquiry	⟶	Research-Based Core Program & Interventions

build a house starting with the roof—and without a proper foundation, no structure can stand.

Assessing Your Current Reality

In *Good to Great*, Jim Collins (2005, p. 74) states that "the first step of leadership is not visioning, but rather confronting the brutal facts." When building a PRTI, a school must be willing to assess honestly the current reality of its core program. This, not a successful intervention system, is PRTI's most important component, for the core program does more to ensure students' success than the most comprehensive system of supplemental supports. Therefore, schools should first strive to teach "right" the first time. No PRTI can fully compensate for poor initial instruction.

To assess your site's core program, first consider the following questions:

- Is learning the fundamental purpose of your school?

- Do teams have frequent collaboration time embedded into the professional day?

- Do learning goals drive each team's work?

- Have teacher teams clearly defined student learning outcomes for each grade level and/or course of study?

- Do teams collaborate to create and administer timely and common formative assessments?

- Does your school know which students have not mastered specific essential standards?

- Does your common assessment data identify strengths and weaknesses in core instructional practices?

Identify Under-Represented Students

Once a school has honestly and thoroughly assessed its core program's effectiveness, it should be able not only to validate what is working, but also to identify which students are not succeeding. We refer to these children as *under-represented* students. Educators may know these students as *at risk*, but that term implies there is something wrong with the student. In fact, these students are more accurately described as *under-represented*—their parents may not sufficiently represent their needs, and the school may not recognize and provide supports. Because PRTIs are created to provide additional learning time and support to students who have not succeeded in core programs, specific student needs should drive the design of interventions. There are three ways to identify under-represented students:

1. Teachers and other school staff (for example, counselors or administrators) recommend students.

2. Students receive low scores in such summative assessment data as end-of-year statewide standardized tests.

3. Formative assessments help educators identify students who have not mastered a set of power standards or who have failed to make expected progress toward mastery.

Schools will be most successful in taking advantage of these information sources if they develop structures to facilitate data gathering. Commercially produced or staff-created data-warehousing and data-mining tools can help organize and analyze areas of relative student weakness. Clear data is key to helping student-study, grade-level, content-area, and other teams discuss student work and performance. Schools must have assessments and criteria for identifying students at risk of failure and an opportunity to analyze these students' needs.

Find Resources

Building a PRTI requires a wide range of resources. Because schools expend discretionary funds as close to the classroom as possible and in ways that most directly affect student learning, educators must regularly evaluate how existing and new resources—funds, personnel, and programs—positively affect such learning. That is particularly important because every year, schools and districts compete for instructional monies and other resources.

Schools should ask such questions as:

• Is the supplemental art program more important than a targeted, research-based comprehension program?

• Are new computers more critical than a part-time, trained paraprofessional who will help kindergarten and first graders with their phonemic awareness skills?

- Are conferences more important than release time for teachers to help them collaboratively design common assessments and analyze student work?

If building a PRTI system is a priority, it must be the focus of school expenditures. Newly purchased programs and recently hired personnel must contribute to supporting students' learning. When funds are limited, their efficient use matters a great deal. Two programs that are research-based and that prove equally effective may have very different price tags. Budget constraints may also determine how many students a PRTI serves.

Periodically, schools may need to revisit their decisions about how to use personnel most effectively. For example, a school might determine that paraprofessionals should deliver explicit reading or mathematics programs instead of monitoring students' learning of sight words or helping teachers to staple or make copies of papers. Likewise, instead of employing an additional secretary or assistant principal, schools may need to engage a reading or mathematics specialist.

Schools must be both creative and fiscally prudent in selecting programs for their PRTI system. Historically, special education has utilized programs that have a strong research base, even when students may lack a diagnosed need in the area that the program targets. These programs should be adapted and reformulated for *targeted* intervention.

Similarly, though districts regularly acquire quality programs for learners at risk, these programs often gather dust in a district office warehouse. Teachers may find the proposed interventions too difficult to implement, or they may not have made a commitment to assist all learners. Schools should inquire whether their district already has stockpiled programs for free use before purchasing new ones.

Evaluate programs using the following criteria:

- Is it systematic, research-based, and explicit?

- Can a paraprofessional deliver the instruction?

- Is the initiative computer-based?

- Does it provide a targeted, supplemental intervention or a broad intervention that supplants a core curriculum?

- What is the optimal number of students in an instructional group using the program?

When calculating costs for technology-based interventions, schools should consider the personnel required to deliver intervention programs, as well as their computer, internet connectivity, and technical support needs. Although pyramid response to intervention may require new programs, the newest, most expensive, and flashiest programs may not be the best.

Next Steps

As this chapter has shown, before building a pyramid response to intervention, you must first embrace the need for change, assess your current core program in terms of PLC best practices, identify under-represented students, and brainstorm all the potential resources you might use for students who are struggling. Only then are you ready to evaluate the effectiveness of your current interventions. A schoolwide, systematic PRTI is only as effective as the specific interventions that comprise it. The next chapter focuses on the characteristics of highly effective interventions.

Have you created a foundation for your PRTI by implementing the essential characteristics of a professional learning community?

See page 175 for "Creating a PLC Foundation," an activity to help assess your current reality in implementing PLC essential characteristics and set short- and long-term goals for improvement.

See page 176 for "Creating a Learning Mission," a step-by-step protocol for creating a collective mission statement.

See page 177 for "Identifying Essential Standards," a powerful graphic organizer with guiding questions that will assist your team in identifying essential learning standards.

Continues on page 58→

See page 180 for "Unpacking the Standards," an activity to help your team dig deeply into essential standards.

See page 181 for "Common Formative Assessments," an activity to help your team understand the characteristics of effective common formative assessments.

See page 183 for "Common Assessment Desired Outcomes," a protocol to help teams analyze common assessment data and apply the findings to create effective, targeted interventions.

Who are your under-represented students?

See page 184 for an activity that will help your leadership team identify your under-represented students—those students who are not being adequately successful in your core program.

What are your human and fiscal resources?

See page 185 for an activity designed to guide your school in brainstorming all the possible resources that you can marshal to support interventions for under-represented students.

Visit **go.solution-tree.com/rti**
to download these activities.

Chapter Five

Learning CPR

The educated differ from the uneducated as much as the living from the dead.

—Aristotle

*M*aple Elementary School was located in a remote area in the Pacific Northwest; most of the students' parents had attended Maple themselves, and staff members knew most children by name even before they started school. Life was uneventful in their small town—until the day the attendance secretary entered the principal's office and announced with a concerned voice, "Amy Johnson is suffering a severe asthma attack in PE; we think she's lost consciousness." Recognizing the urgency of the situation, the principal first instructed the secretary to call 911 immediately and then rushed to the gymnasium. There, he noted that the site crisis team was already working to assist the student in need and the school nurse was administering cardiopulmonary resuscitation (CPR); the physical education teacher was clearing the area of on-looking students, and a designated member of the crisis team was waiting at the front of the school to guide the ambulance crew to the correct location.

Within minutes, paramedics arrived, assessed Amy's condition, and provided her with targeted, lifesaving medical treatment. Soon, Amy regained consciousness. After a few tense minutes, the fire chief said confidently, "She's breathing on her own now; she's going to be just fine."

Later that afternoon, the principal attended a parent-teacher meeting regarding Robbie, a sixth-grade student whose family had just moved to Maple's small town. The meeting opened with a review of Robbie's educational history. Previous report cards painted a clear, consistent picture: Robbie was a remedial reader who had difficulty decoding words and retaining information. Each year, this deficiency grew, and as it did, his attention in class and overall effort waned. While previous teachers' comments described Robbie's learning difficulties, little documentation existed on what interventions they had employed to support him.

Robbie's current teacher said, "He's not trying at all in class, and until he starts to care about school, ask for help, and work harder at his assignments, he's going to continue to fail." His parents threw up their hands in frustration at her words.

"We've tried motivating Robbie for years," his mother said, "but nothing seems to work." The meeting ended with the team deciding to allow Robbie to experience a "fresh start" at Maple Elementary and to meet again when the semester ended in 9 weeks to review his progress.

That evening, the principal sat in his office thinking about the day's events. He had faced two student emergencies, a medical and an educational crisis, which ended with opposite outcomes. Staff had been successful with Amy, the asthmatic girl, because they were guided by an extreme sense of urgency; everyone understood that she faced a life-or-death situation. Maple had developed and practiced a systematic emergency response plan, so it was prepared to respond to Amy's health needs. Their response was timely, directive, and administered by trained professionals. In the end, by providing CPR, paramedics saved Amy's life.

But when it came to Robbie, the struggling learner, Maple's staff lacked a sense of urgency at the parent conference. There was no systematic program that would provide Robbie with timely, targeted, and directive learning help. Thus, while being gratifyingly successful with the asthmatic girl, the team at Maple was frustratingly ineffective with the boy who was educationally at risk.

An Appropriate Response to Learning Emergencies

Unfortunately, Robbie's story is fairly representative of the vast majority of U.S. schools. Nearly all schools are well-prepared to respond to medical emergencies but woefully unprepared to handle learning crises. Worse, most schools lack a real sense of urgency in addressing student learning problems. Yet the only real difference between the life-threatening conditions of the asthmatic girl and the educational crisis of the boy who was significantly below grade-level in reading is the speed with which they are "dying."

To successfully help learners at risk, we must apply the same characteristics of our medical emergency response procedures to our instructional intervention program. In other words, we must provide our students at risk with "Learning CPR," which is:

- Urgent
- Directive
- Timely
- Targeted
- Administered by trained professionals
- Systematic

Urgent

An effective intervention program starts with a sense of pressing need. Beyond the high-stakes school accountability requirements mandated by state and federal laws, the difference between success and failure in school is, quite literally, life and death for our students. Today, a child who graduates from school with a mastery of essential skills and knowledge is prepared to compete in the global marketplace, with numerous paths of opportunity available to lead a happy and successful life. Yet for students who fail in our educational system, the reality is that there are virtually no paths of opportunity. A century ago, students who failed in school could secure a manufacturing or agricultural job that required few prior skills but provided sufficient wages and benefits; today, these jobs are either nonexistent or fail to pay above poverty-level compensation. Consequently, the likely pathway for these students is an adult life of hardship, incarceration, and/or dependence on society's welfare systems. Children who are not reading at grade level by age 9 are 10 times more likely to drop out of school before receiving a high school diploma. In turn, these students will earn on average about $12,000 per year, nearly 50% less than those who have a high school diploma (Levin, Belfield, Muenning, & Rouse, 2007). In addition, 43% of people with the lowest literacy skills live below the government's official poverty line (Roberts, 1998). According to the report *Literacy Behind Prison Walls,* 70% of all prison inmates are functionally illiterate or read below a fourth-grade level; this number rises above 80% in the juvenile justice system (Haigler, Harlow, O'Connor, & Campbell, 1994).

Because students who fail within our educational system face such severe and sobering consequences, it is incomprehensible that most traditional schools respond to students at risk with a defeated or laissez-faire attitude. In contrast, once a school makes student learning its fundamental mission, it manifests a sense of professional and moral urgency to do whatever it takes to ensure that all students succeed. This sense of urgency should be the driving force behind a pyramid response to intervention.

Directive

By making an intervention voluntary, a school in effect tells students that success—and failure—are optional. If a school's core mission is student learning, then learning should never be optional. As adults, we understand the long-term consequences of educational failure far better than our students do. We should never allow them to embark upon that path.

Consider the case of a middle school that offered an extensive after-school tutorial program open to all students. The school administration, which was very proud of this intervention, noted that its faculty provided more than 30 support sessions a week, covering all subject areas, at a cost of almost $40,000 a year.

Eager to learn from this model, a visitation team attended some tutorial sessions. By the end of its visit, the team noticed that almost all the children who attended the help sessions appeared to be high-achieving students. Asked about this, teachers confirmed the team's observation. One educator summed it up best by commenting, "Of course all the high achievers are here—that's how they get such high grades. It's really a shame that our at-risk students almost never attend, because boy, do they need it!"

Contrast this to the behavior of the paramedics; when they assisted Amy, the asthma victim, they did not *offer* her the opportunity for medical assistance, but rather immediately assessed her condition and then *provided* direct help. Similarly, education professionals must do more than offer students at risk extra help and support. Considering the lifelong consequences for academic failure, we must *require* and *ensure* that they receive prompt and effective assistance.

Timely

An intervention program is only effective when the school responds *promptly* if students do not learn and provides them additional time to master essential skills and content.

Allowing sufficient time is critical to student learning. We know that virtually every student can learn at a high level if we provide him or her with targeted instruction and sufficient time to learn.

A Formula for Learning

Targeted Instruction + Time = Learning

Targeted instruction is defined as highly effective teaching practices that meet each child's individual learning needs. Because learning needs vary for each student, so will what is considered effective instruction for him or her. For example, consider the learning needs of a gifted student who is a native English speaker and those of a non-native speaker who recently immigrated to the United States. English-language learner instruction, which would be inappropriate for native English speakers, might be very effective for the non-native speakers.

Like instruction, the time allocated for learning must be matched to each student's needs. We know that toddlers do not learn to walk or talk at the same rate; similarly, students do not learn to read, write, or solve equations at the same time.

Formula for Learning: Traditional School

Targeted Instruction + Time = Learning

        ↓   ↓   ↓

   Constant   **Constant** **Variable**

Unfortunately, many traditional schools implement a formula for learning that guarantees that some students will *not* learn. In part, this is because these schools primarily provide whole-group instruction, which translates into a "one-size-fits-all" program. Failure to differentiate instruction to meet individual student needs makes the mode of instruction a constant in the learning formula. Compounding the problem, many schools create rigid pacing guides and lesson plans that allot a specific amount of time for students to learn new material, thus making time a constant. In contrast, the formula for learning that we suggest makes learning a constant, while time allotted and mode of instruction are variable.

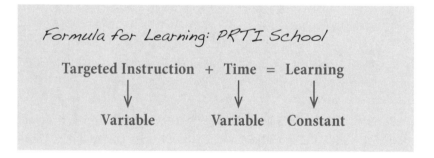

Formula for Learning: PRTI School

Targeted Instruction + Time = Learning

        ↓   ↓   ↓

   Variable   **Variable**   **Constant**

Traditional schools "leave students behind" because their formula for learning practically ensures this outcome. But if a school's mission is to help *all* students achieve high levels of learning, then *learning* must become the constant, while instruction and time become variables.

When creating a PRTI, Tier 1 instruction and supplemental interventions must be carefully designed to differentiate teaching practices based upon student needs and to provide flexible time for students to demonstrate mastery.

In addition to offering more time to learn, an effective intervention program must respond *promptly* when students do not learn. At traditional schools, staff usually monitor student progress at the midpoint and end of each grading period, and provide quarterly and end-of-term report cards to students and their parents that indicate the student's academic standing in each course of study. This practice contains two innate problems. First, schools that merely *notify* parents of a student's failing progress are not providing an intervention. Instead, they should delineate specific actions they will undertake to provide the student additional support. Second, most grading period intervals represent 25–50% of the grading term. Struggling students can fall so far behind peers during this period that it may be too late to effectively help them catch up.

In a schoolwide PRTI system, educators frequently monitor students' progress and modify the interventions they provide at least every 3 weeks. Again, as with the unconscious asthma student on the gym floor, a timely response can make the difference between life and death.

Targeted

CPR restored Amy's breathing and ultimately saved her life. Yet CPR clearly is not the right response for all health ailments. If a medical professional were to administer CPR to someone suffering a severe cold, that person might suffer more or even die. In educational interventions, as in medical ones, professionals' responses need to be targeted to each individual's specific situation.

Students fail to achieve for many reasons. Some students lack the prior skills needed to master new curriculum; some students need additional time and practice to learn essential concepts; some students receive initial teaching that does not meet their instructional needs; still other students fail to give the effort needed to succeed. Each of these unique causes requires a specific, targeted response. All too often, schools create broadly focused interventions, grouping struggling students together by the common symptom of failure rather than by the cause of their difficulties. This would be like an emergency room diagnosing all patients as "sick," then prescribing the same remedy of penicillin to all of them. By chance, the treatment may work for some. But as a whole, the hospital will still have a room full of sick patients, and staff will have wasted a lot of medicine.

When a student is struggling, the school's goal should not be to do *something*, but to do the *right thing*. Staff must first diagnose a student's needs and then provide a targeted response to meet them. The more targeted the intervention, the more likely it is to be effective.

Administered by Trained Professionals

When faced with a life-threatening crisis, we depend on trained professionals to respond. In fact, the more urgent the medical need, the more important this professional's services are. For example, someone suffering from the flu usually sees the family physician, while a cancer patient visits an oncologist. In designing an effective intervention program, we need to apply this same guiding principle.

Douglas Reeves' research (2007) concludes that one of a school's most effective learning strategies is to have highly trained teachers work with the students most at risk. Unfortunately, the vast majority of schools do the exact opposite: New teachers receive the most difficult teaching assignments, while veteran educators work almost exclusively with students who are high achieving. Traditional school culture honors a seniority system in which more tenured teachers earn the right to work with students who are high achieving, while new teachers must "pay their dues" with children who are middle and low achieving. School administrators usually support this system because parents of the most successful students often complain when their children get the new teacher, while parents of under-represented students rarely voice this concern.

Ultimately, most schools end up doing the equivalent of sending patients with cold symptoms to the brain surgeon, and patients with brain tumors to a medical intern. In a PRTI system, decisions are based foremost upon their impact on learning, instead of on seniority or parental concerns. The best-planned intervention program will fail if outstanding educators do not implement it.

Systematic

While a life-threatening medical emergency on campus is a relatively uncommon event, the planning of systematic response to such a crisis is not. If the same asthma emergency described occurred at schools in Maine, Missouri, or Montana, their ways of handling the crisis almost certainly would be very similar. While medical emergency response systems are always prepared to provide critical care, few schools have developed effective response systems for students who are struggling academically. Instead, traditional schools have developed an educational "lottery system" of support. When a student is fortunate enough to be assigned to teachers who provide extra time and effort, he or she gets the help and support needed. But when a child is placed in a class with an educator who lacks the same level of expertise or commitment to learning, the student probably will receive no additional academic support and so will lose the educational lottery.

Schools that focus on learning provide students additional time and support *by design*, not by chance or luck. A systematic approach to interventions, as used in a PRTI, is not an auxiliary program that exists outside the regular core program. Instead, it is a vital, sequential part of the instructional program that provides additional time and support to any student demonstrating the need.

Traditional Responses to Learning Emergencies

Regrettably, the characteristics of an effective intervention program—urgent, directive, timely, targeted, administered by trained professionals, and systematic—are rarely part of the traditional interventions that most schools employ. Some examples of traditional ways of handling educational crises include:

- Individual teacher response
- Remedial classes
- Summer school
- Retention
- Alternative and special education
- Doing nothing

Individual Teacher Response

In most schools, the first and often only intervention is to leave it up to individual teachers to respond to the needs of their struggling students. With a battle cry of "leave no child behind," classroom instructors are prompted with educational catch-phrases like "Be data-driven" and "Differentiate." Yet within a traditional school culture in which teachers work in isolation, it is virtually impossible for every teacher to possess all the knowledge, skills, and time necessary to meet the individual needs of all his or her students. Every day, the vast majority of educators teach the very best way they know how—so after they have initially taught an essential concept, what is the likelihood that they have a more effective way to reteach the concept to their failing students? Most teachers reteach using the same instructional practices that failed to work the first time. Even if teachers did possess all the knowledge and skills necessary, would they have the time and resources to achieve these ends, when they are still equally responsible for meeting the needs of their students who *did* master essential concepts the first time? Assuming as much, how logical is it for a school to base its intervention program on this isolated response?

Remedial Classes

When a teacher's response to a student's learning difficulty proves ineffective, most traditional schools conclude that the child lacks the prerequisite skills needed to be successful in the class. In response, the school often assigns the student to a remedial course of study. In reality, all the school has done is to "lower the bar," thus offering the child virtually no chance of accelerating learning to close his or her achievement gap.

For example, if a student is struggling in a grade-appropriate algebra course, a traditional school might conclude that the child lacks prealgebra skills and place him or her in a remedial program to learn them. While the student is in this program, his or her classmates continue to study algebra, and the child's learning gap with peers continues to widen. Over time, the struggling student's ability to compete in nearly all post–high school academic and professional opportunities will steadily diminish and ultimately end.

A common special education practice that diminishes a student's access to rigorous learning standards is the misuse of IEP goals and modifications. Frequently, when a student with special needs is having difficulties meeting grade-level standards, either the child's IEP goals are revised or classroom modifications are implemented, ultimately creating a new course of study that is below grade level. For a professional learning community, this differentiated approach to struggling students undermines its mission to ensure high levels of learning for all children. To assist children who need remedial instruction, a school that focuses on learning will design interventions that complement and support, not replace, students' participation in rigorous curricula.

Summer School

While almost every American school offers summer classes, little evidence exists of their effectiveness in improving learning for students at risk. That is unsurprising, for consider this intervention's underlying premise: Students who have failed in a regular full-day program for the entire school year will catch up after a few weeks of partial-day remediation. At best, summer school provides an opportunity for high school students to make up the coursework needed for graduation. But even in this case, these students probably will leave summer school without mastery of the essential learning they need. Given the human and fiscal resources summer school requires, students' net gain in learning hardly seems to justify the expense.

Retention

In this age of high standards and accountability, many schools tout retention as an effective intervention. At the surface level, it seems logical that students should not be promoted to the next grade until they have mastered the essential standards of their current grade level. Yet research shows that students who repeat a grade prior to high school have a markedly higher risk of dropping out of high school than those students who are continuously promoted through school (Moller & Stearns, 2008). And along with the negative social consequences, the retained student usually receives the same ineffective instructional program as the previous year. Retention assumes that what did not work the first time will be the answer to the student's needs.

True, there are times when retention is appropriate. But if an intervention program seeks to help struggling students learn and succeed in school, it makes no sense to depend on a practice that has proven so counterproductive.

Alternative and Special Education

When a student fails to benefit from traditional interventions, many schools conclude that he or she either is learning disabled or unable to succeed in a comprehensive school program and so should be placed in an "alternative" one. Instead of looking internally to evaluate and revise the instructional program, many schools look externally, placing blame for a child's failed learning on his or her inability to adjust to, comprehend, and function well in the school's core curriculum.

While special education testing yields some useful information about the student, it rarely evaluates the instructional program that he or she has received, nor does it usually lead to an effective intervention plan. More than 98% of all special education students never reach a level of improvement that qualifies them for redesignation (IDEIA, 2004). Imagine how most parents would respond if told that their child's special education IEP plan had less than a 2% chance of returning him or her to the regular education program! This is not meant as an indictment of special education. However, as professionals, we must be willing to look at the hard facts of a system that is not working for most students.

Doing Nothing

Tragically, one of the most common school responses to students who are struggling is really a nonintervention: to do nothing. Thousands of schools across North America lack discernable, targeted programs to help struggling students. By merely providing students the opportunity to learn, the school holds them alone accountable for choosing to succeed or fail. These schools may claim that they are teaching children "responsibility" for their choices, thus preparing them for the "real world." In reality, they are allowing their students to follow a highly destructive path with long-term consequences. It is doubtful these educators would allow their own children to fail. On the other hand, a PRTI will hold *all* of its students accountable to a single outcome—high levels of learning.

Considering how ineffective most traditional interventions are, one wonders why they are so prevalent. Unfortunately, many educational institutions confuse *longstanding practice* with *best practice*. Just because a particular instructional program has been used for decades does not necessarily make it "tried and true." After all, for more than 2,000 years, bloodletting was considered medical best practice for most ailments. But today, we would not consider applying leeches to an asthma victim because we know that this medical procedure is not considered best practice.

While many traditional interventions are largely ineffective in practice, they could become highly effective if redesigned to align with the essential characteristics of "Learning CPR." For example, what if the middle school with the after-school tutoring program made it *mandatory* for students at risk? With this proviso, the program would become much more broadly utilized and thus effective in assisting students who need it most. Likewise, carefully targeted summer school classes that are taught by highly trained teachers could provide students the additional instructional support they need to learn essential standards.

In the end, a schoolwide, systematic PRTI will only be as effective as the specific interventions that comprise it. A school that builds a PRTI with ineffective interventions assures that all students have equal access to a system of failure. Once a school staff has aligned their interventions with the characteristics of Learning CPR, then they are prepared to begin building a PRTI.

Are your current interventions aligned with the essential characteristics of Learning CPR?

See page 186 for "Evaluating Our Current Interventions," an activity to help you evaluate your interventions and align them with the essential characteristics of Learning CPR.

Visit **go.solution-tree.com/rti**
to download this activity.

Chapter Six

Tier 1: The Core Program

In times of profound change, the learners inherit the earth, while the learned find themselves beautifully equipped to deal with a world that no longer exists.

—Al Rogers, pioneer in long-distance learning

Built in the 1960s, Oak Elementary School was once surrounded by single-family homes and cornfields. Most of Oak's students were white, English-speaking, and from middle-class families. Through the years, the school gained a well-deserved reputation in the community for educational excellence. However, in the 1990s, the district radically altered Oak's attendance area. The new boundaries encompassed an area comprised almost exclusively of low-income, high-density apartments populated by factory workers in a nearby city. Oak's demographics now were reversed; a vast majority of its students were economically disadvantaged, minority, and English-language learners.

Within a year of the boundary changes, most students were scoring below proficiency in reading, writing, and mathematics on state achievement tests. Individual teachers worked tirelessly, but unfortunately, their teaching practices, which had been highly successful under the old demographics, proved ineffective with the school's new students. Teachers referred struggling students to intervention programs, but with so many students at risk, these services quickly were overwhelmed.

Threatened with state sanctions, the school staff completed a self-study, which concluded that Oak's primary problem was not a lack of interventions, but rather a systemic problem throughout the school's entire culture and instructional program. In other words, Oak did not need a new program; it needed a whole new way of doing business.

Strengthening the Core Program

As the staff at Oak Elementary learned, no intervention program can compensate for ineffective core instructional practices. For this reason, a pyramid response to intervention must be built upon the framework of a school's core instructional program. *Core program*, also commonly referred to as *Tier 1, base, primary,* or *universal* program, refers to a school's initial instructional practices—in other words, the teaching and school experiences that all kids receive every day.

Intervention models are based on the assumption that a school's core program will almost exclusively meet the educational needs of at least 75% of its students. *A school that has significantly less than 75% of its students at or above grade-level proficiency has a core program problem, not an intervention problem.*

Differentiate Instruction

The most important step a school can take to improve its core program is differentiating instruction and small-group activities. Schools must first ensure that exceptional and committed teachers are delivering research-based core programs as intended and using classwide formative assessment data to identify emerging classwide areas of need. A Tier 1 curriculum must be prioritized so that students have ample opportunity to master power standards. The core program also must include a component that specializes instruction and learning based on individuals' and small groups' disparate needs.

Many elementary and secondary programs do not include structured, consistent, differentiated segments as part of their core program, but they should. Before schools prescribe Tier 2 (supplemental) or Tier 3 (intensive) interventions, classroom teachers must differentiate instruction for small groups of students in the classroom. These small groups may meet with their teacher several times a week. Some students may require a thorough review of information that was previously taught to the entire class. Others may need instruction that extends and enriches prior lessons, adding depth and complexity to the curriculum. Still others may need a flexible combination of remediation and enrichment, as formative diagnoses dictate.

Two challenges that schools face when upgrading the quality of their teaching within the Tier 1 program are classroom management and the selection of quality activities that students can complete independently. Clear, structured classroom management practices that students have thoroughly practiced must be present for differentiated instruction to work well. For a teacher to productively work with a small group of the students in the class, the rest of the class must be deeply and quietly engaged in a high-quality independent activity.

For example, suppose that during a 2-hour literacy block, the teacher and *all* students interact in phonics, fluency, and decoding exercises. Together, they read a short story, focusing on applying appropriate comprehension strategies and skills. Following this, the students engage in small-group learning for 60 80 minutes, a period of time designed to reinforce literacy skills.

The teacher structures this block so that students engage in meaningful learning, particularly when they are in the small, homogenous groups that she leads. They have a list of "must-do's," which include sorting their spelling words, reading their decodable and assigned stories with a buddy, working on editing their current piece of writing, and completing their grammar practice worksheets. In addition, students can work on "may-dos," which include completing math and reading practice on websites that are bookmarked on a classroom computer, or independently reading or writing in their journals.

Meanwhile, the teacher selects students to work with her at a small table, where they practice sight words, review the decoding skills of the week, or collaboratively participate in reciprocal reading groups. Groups may last from 15–20 minutes, and membership may change from day to day, or even week to week; some students may participate in several groups.

In Tier 1, then, educators meet individual student needs by differentiating the support and time they offer. If they need further support (Tier 2 or Tier 3), a specialist may pull students in small groups for a 20–25 minute intervention session, usually when the students would otherwise be working independently. Students receiving additional interventions don't miss differentiated time with their classroom teachers.

Determine Power Standards

State departments of education determine standards that school districts must meet, with selected standards in some content more heavily represented on end-of-the-year tests than others. In other cases, districts and individual schools must engage in a process of determining which standards are most critical.

Doug Reeves (2005) specifies three criteria to help educators determine which standards deserve a higher priority: endurance, leverage, and necessity for the next level of instruction.

Endurance—Does the standard address knowledge and skills that will endure throughout a student's academic career and professional life?

Leverage—Does it address knowledge and skills that will be of value in multiple content areas?

Necessity—Does it provide the essential knowledge and skills that students need to succeed in the next grade level?

As Robert Marzano (2003) makes clear, students cannot be expected to master all the standards that most state curricula have. He estimates that students would need to attend school for an additional decade, through the "22nd grade," to learn them adequately. Marzano recommends that educators reduce by two thirds the number of standards in most content-area documents that delineate standards. *Depth*, meaning student mastery of the material that teachers cover, is more important than *breadth*, the extent of the information and skills that they teach.

Once a team of teachers has prioritized standards, they can enhance the core program by further analyzing and deconstructing these standards for a single grade level or a particular course during a 1-hour staff meeting or during collaboration time. In one method, the team first writes each grade-level standard for a particular content area on a large piece of paper. Next, they cut out released items from state tests and paste them under the standard to which they correspond. This step takes some discussion to make sense of the standards. A deeper understanding of standards will improve lessons and the Tier 1 program.

After this discussion, teachers analyze the way the test questions relate to the standards and the concepts that underlie them. Finally, teachers rewrite the standard in teacher-friendly and student-friendly language. This simple process can help teachers and, ultimately, students more completely understand the essential questions and concepts that they must master. (See page 180 for a reproducible exercise on unpacking standards.)

Analyze Assessment Data

Summative and formative assessment data about students, including their course grades, can inform staff about the quality of the core program. *Summative assessments* typically occur at the end of the unit. While they evaluate student learning, such assessments are not intended to be used to modify future instruction or diagnose student needs. *Formative assessments* are diagnostic progress-monitoring tools that are used to adjust teaching and learning while they are still occurring. Thus, summative tests are assessments *of* learning, and formative tests are assessments *for* learning.

If summative end-of-course or end-of-year test results indicate that most students are below proficiency, the core program must be re-examined. *Educators who rely on interventions alone to meet the needs of students who score below proficiency will never solve the basic problem these children face.* In fact, if a school does not address the core program's effectiveness, roughly the same percentage of students will require interventions year after year.

Likewise, if a large number of students are receiving D's or F's on assignments, and teachers do not use that formative assessment data to adjust classroom instruction and curriculum, interventions will probably prove insufficient for many students. Similarly, when a large percentage of students score poorly on such instruments as DIBELS and the Qualitative Reading Inventory, the core program has not been serving them well.

By carefully analyzing summative assessment data, educators can identify specific areas of the core program that need the most attention. Formative assessments reveal what each student needs within the core program, which in turn helps inform a differentiated curriculum. Schools that wish to maximize their core programs' effectiveness will diagnose student needs and prescribe carefully designed solutions that can be delivered in the Tier 1 program, perhaps during differentiated workshop or small-group time.

Ensure Quality Teaching and Focused Staff Development

The quality of the classroom teacher is the most significant factor in maximizing student learning. The principal, as instructional leader on campus, should guide a higher quality of education by observing teachers, ensuring that they address the school's two or three focused goals, and monitoring whether students are engaged in learning. In addition, principals and other educators must see to it that staff meetings focus on the types of professional development that can improve teaching and student performance, as specified by the learning goals that the staff has agreed upon.

In his investigation of 90/90/90 schools, Doug Reeves (2000) identified and analyzed five attributes that inform quality teaching, focus staff development needs, and produce superior core programs:

1. *Academic achievement*—All stakeholders, as their first priority, work to help students achieve academic mastery and other growth.

2. *Curriculum choices*—Teachers spend more time on core subjects (reading, writing, and mathematics) and less on other content areas; depth/mastery of key subjects is favored over breadth/coverage of all areas.

3. *Frequent assessment and opportunity for improvement*— Educators frequently monitor student progress and require, not invite, students to constantly improve their performance.

4. *Writing*—Children write often, particularly on performance assessments, and educators teach good writing skills, model them, and help children practice their writing across content areas.

5. *External scoring*—Teachers grade work from other teachers' students, principals grade students' work from teachers at their school, and one school's teachers grade another school's student work. Most importantly, educators analyze student performance for the purpose of improving teaching and learning.

Quality teaching makes a difference; teaching of the highest quality is focused on key content and focused on depth over breadth.

Maximize Instructional Time

Marzano's (2003) 22nd grade estimate assumes that 100% of classroom time would be used for instruction, but in actuality, he ascertains, teachers utilize only 21–69% of classroom time for instruction. This shows how critical it is to take advantage of every moment students are in school. Teachers must begin learning activities the moment students enter the classroom and ensure that they continue learning until the very end of the period; educators must also create fluid transitions between activities.

Use Programs With Fidelity

Using adopted programs with *fidelity*—the way they were designed to be used—accomplishes two things: First, it prevents gaps within and between curricular components. By following the scope and sequence designed by the curriculum's researchers and writers, students have the best opportunity to master the standards addressed. Second, fidelity helps educators evaluate the efficacy of adopted programs in improving student learning; if you have not implemented the program as intended, you cannot accurately evaluate its results.

Maximizing instructional time requires staff to examine each lesson and all classwork and to ask the following questions:

- Are students actively engaged in work related to prioritized power standards?

- What is the best way to ensure students achieve mastery?

- Are we using the most efficient way of helping students to learn?

Tier 1 in Elementary Schools

Student learning is the critical yardstick by which a school's success is measured. However, in too many schools, teaching is not explicit and purposeful, and thus student learning is incidental. Often, only those students with the prerequisite skills and family supports for learning thrive, while under-represented students who lack such skills and supports fall through the cracks. In these schools, classroom time and teacher support are constants while learning is a variable.

At Knob Hill Elementary School in San Marcos, California, all ethnic subgroups of students perform at very high levels. This diverse school has helped students—nearly half of whom are economically poor—beat the odds by upgrading its core program. The school provides a solid academic program early in kindergarten and first grade, and offers all children who need it a thorough review of the core program within the instructional day. In so doing, Knob Hill has improved the performance of its kindergarten and first-grade students by nearly 50% over 2 years.

By narrowly concentrating on the core content in writing, reading, and mathematics, students attained mastery of foundational concepts while keeping critical thinking as the primary goal. Knob Hill also focuses its resources by insisting that the curriculum used in the core program be designed to enhance student learning. Finally, the site sets high expectations for students and celebrates when educators and students achieve excellence.

In Dana Point, California, Richard Henry Dana Elementary School focuses on strengthening the core, resulting in multiple state awards for a school in which 78% of students qualify for free lunch. Teachers focus on reading, writing, and mathematics, subjects that take up 80–85% of the instructional time each day. The staff ensure coverage of all aspects of a balanced literacy curriculum; they use the chosen curriculum with fidelity, identify power standards in mathematics, and commit to significant student writing every day, with a focus on key genres and applications.

R. H. Dana screens all students at least three times a year and further assesses those children who read below grade level. Grade-level teacher teams design common assessments that the teachers collaboratively grade or use commercially produced unit assessments that both reveal gaps between classwide learning and grade-level learning goals and identify children who need additional time and support.

Professional development at R. H. Dana focuses on helping teachers improve their instruction in reading, writing, and mathematics; maximize instructional time; identify power standards; and analyze student work. The school's focused approach has resulted in improving student learning.

In 2 years, students reaching proficiency on state reading tests increased from 30% to 48%.

Tier 1 in Middle Schools

Twin Peaks Middle School, a successful middle school in a large school district in Poway, California, uses its fall benchmark reading assessments to help improve student performance in core English and social studies classes throughout the year. The assessments provide Lexile levels for each student, thus identifying a range of text difficulty that students can read independently. (Lexiles are numbers from 0 to 2,000 that denote both reading ability and text difficulty.) Teachers collaboratively determine the Lexile levels of the core texts that they will use in the classroom, matching students' Lexile levels to the Lexiles of the core program's textbook; then they determine the levels for supplementary materials that will enhance the core in differentiated small groups. For example, in social studies classrooms, some learners lack the reading skills to access the core text. The teacher can utilize Untied Streaming (a subscription-based repository of instructional resources) to preview social studies concepts with these students so that they are more successful when they later attempt to comprehend the text by themselves. The teacher meets with a small group of these learners while others work independently. What results is a stronger program as teachers better utilize the Tier 1 curriculum and differentiate instruction within the classroom.

Teachers at Marco Forster Middle School in San Juan Capistrano, California, used to assign zeroes to students who had failed exams and didn't offer them the opportunity to review and retake tests. The instructors also didn't allow students to turn in missing work for credit, didn't return corrected unit tests, and barred students from retaking these exams to demonstrate increased levels of mastery. In time, the staff came to realize that these practices conflicted with their goal of setting high expectations and doing whatever it takes to help students learn. In short, teachers recognized that their job was not to teach, but to ensure that students learn.

Today, teachers at Marco Forster expect students to complete all work and give partial or full credit for previously missed assignments. After teachers give unit assessments, they organize lunchtime or after-school sessions to allow a student to review a test (a parent's signature confirms that the child has had this opportunity) and subsequently to retake a modified version, with slightly different problems that assess the same content. This process allows the student to increase mastery of the subject and thus improve his or her grade. The school creates multiple versions of tests, each with its own questions, so that teachers can pass them back to students for review.

The results are impressive. The school culture at Marco Forster now focuses on student mastery of essential skills and material; teachers, students, and parents view failure as unacceptable, and students take greater responsibility for their own learning; consequently, student learning has improved. The percent of students passing state tests has increased by 10%, and the number of students receiving F grades on their report cards has been reduced by 75% over 3 years.

Tier 1 in High Schools

The math resource teacher in the Capistrano Unified School District, a large district south of Los Angeles, has worked with high school math departments to analyze state standards using the method described in the section on power standards earlier in this chapter. During their collaboration time, math teachers place cut-out released items from state tests and attach them to butcher paper on which the state math standards are written. After teachers understand these standards, they can better prioritize what content to use and otherwise can focus their instruction. By developing test questions that use a format and language similar to those on state tests, they also are better able to help students perform well on those tests.

Capistrano Valley High School in Mission Viejo made a commitment to the community that it would provide every student with Tier 1 supports. To determine what these interventions would be, the school engaged in a discovery process to create a list of existing supports that its more than 100 teachers provided in their classrooms; this list included only those interventions that every teacher agreed to consistently provide, and was shared with all school families. The school stated that no student—regardless of teacher, grade level, or course—would be allowed to fail. All teachers would provide supports within the regular classroom.

Capistrano Valley also guaranteed that as soon as teachers identified potential student failure in mastering skills or texts, they would send emails or make phone calls until they reached a parent. The school also agreed to provide special time periods for support before school, during lunchtime, or after school.

In addition, all teachers participate in *School Loop*, an individualized report emailed to students and their families at the end of each school day that offers school news, a list of all the student's assignments, and the grade he or she earned in each class. Capistrano Valley mails progress reports to parents of students who have recently received one or more F's at the 3-week mark of each semester and then again every 3 weeks thereafter.

Capistrano Valley staff also explored whether they should add new interventions to the list of supports. They decided to require students to retake exams they had failed, either before or after school, or during lunch. In addition, the school arranged mandatory peer tutoring sessions for students who were failing, using accomplished students from the school's International Baccalaureate program.

Capistrano Valley's existing tutorial program set aside 35 minutes for teachers to provide students with support in specific courses, to participate in enrichment activities, or to learn in a general study hall if such support was unnecessary. After analyzing this program, a process impelled by the school's new commitment to the community, the staff decided that attendance at tutorials would be mandatory when students were failing a class or had any outstanding assignments due. (Students who were failing more than one course were required to go to more than one tutorial a week.) By adding a monitoring component to the tutorial program, the staff also tracked students' attendance and success in raising and maintaining passing grades.

Capistrano Valley's ambitious goals were to ensure that no student was allowed to fail and to guarantee to parents that every teacher would provide a certain set of supports to ensure their children's success. Through their process of discovery and analysis of existing in-class and in-school supports, the school moved closer to guaranteeing that their base program was as sound as possible.

Upgrading the Core Program

As these examples have shown, schools that are committed to improving their Tier 1 core program will:

- Set very high expectations for students and staff.

- Focus their resources, efforts, and curriculum.

- Ensure that all students learn by diagnosing problems and prescribing supports one child at a time.

Set High Expectations

Staff must have high expectations for their own efficacy. The principal must demonstrate that success becomes very likely when educators adequately aid students in their learning. Educators must also have high expectations for one another; positive peer pressure and support can help everyone raise his or her game. The principal can arrange for teachers to share best practices during collaboration time and to observe their peers in action during 30-minute walkthroughs. Most important, staff must have high expectations for students, who must have equally high expectations for themselves. Teachers must genuinely believe and demonstrate that every child can achieve proficiency. Student involvement is critical. Educators should involve students in goal-setting by honestly discussing the results of individual assessments with each student and collaborating to set an improvement goal.

Focus on Instructional Priorities

Instructional leaders provide a focus for the organization's efforts to limit the number of identified prioritized needs to two to four items. In his research on 90/90/90 schools, Reeves (2000) suggests that educators prioritize such key curricular areas as reading, writing, and mathematics; the upgrading of specific student skills in these subjects takes precedence over the coverage of all content areas. Educators should expect and help students to be highly engaged in learning so that they can maximize instructional time. Students can and should be taught how to take responsibility for their own learning by accessing classroom resources when they encounter confusion and by moving independently from one task to another with minimal prompting. To encourage this, teachers must deliver quality instruction that engages students. This may sometimes include direct, explicit, high-quality instruction that gradually releases responsibility through a routine of teacher modeling ("I do it"), guided practice ("we do it"), and independent practice ("you do it"). In addition, schools should prioritize student mastery of power standards. In doing so, sites must utilize with fidelity programs they have recently adopted.

Diagnose and Prescribe

Schools should use a universal screening assessment that provides initial information on which students need additional, specialized support (either Tier 2, if initial assessments reveal skills that are slightly below grade level, or Tier 3, if initial assessments reveal skills that are significantly below grade level) to maximize their learning. This assessment is only step one in the diagnostic process. As individualized student assessments identify more specific needs, staff will increasingly need to develop and deliver differentiated lessons.

Ultimately, however, the most legitimate and effective school improvement effort is *not* to design a system of interventions to help students at risk, but rather to *upgrade the core curriculum.*

What is your Tier 1 core program?

See page 188 for an activity to help your leadership team evaluate your Tier 1 program. Discuss each element that should be found in a Tier 1 program, and honestly record your current reality. Next, record your long-term desired outcome, and establish a few short-term goals.

Visit **go.solution-tree.com/rti**
to download this activity.

Chapter Seven

Tier 2:
The Supplemental Level

*Don't tell me you believe "all kids can learn" . . . tell me
what you're doing about the kids who aren't learning.*

—Richard DuFour

Teresa Sanchez is an experienced language arts teacher at Sequoia Middle School, a large school in a densely populated urban area. At the beginning of the school year, she worked with her fellow English teachers to write a departmental SMART goal that all eighth-grade students demonstrate proficiency on the district's persuasive writing assessment by the end of the school year. (SMART stands for Strategic and Specific, Measurable, Attainable, Results-oriented and Time-bound.)

After giving students the end-of-term persuasive writing assessment, Ms. Sanchez discovered that her teaching of the core curriculum had been very effective; more than 90% of her students demonstrated mastery of this skill.

But some students did not reach proficiency. A few were close to passing the assessment but made slight errors in organization or content; others had not mastered creating a thesis statement; a handful failed to grasp at all the basic concepts of persuasive writing and thus strayed off topic. Finally, some children failed to complete any of the practice assignments or the final essay, so it was impossible to measure their competency.

Reflecting on her students' performance, Ms. Sanchez was perplexed about how to design her future lesson plans. Persuasive writing is critical to success in high school, and she clearly had a number of students who needed supplemental help to reach proficiency. How could she find time to teach a range of topics to some students in need, motivate others who did not try hard, and begin teaching the next essential unit of study to the majority of students that were ready to move on?

Creating Effective Supplements to the Core Program

While the foundation of a PRTI is a highly effective Tier 1 core program, it is virtually impossible for differentiated core instruction alone to meet the needs of every child. Therefore, a learning-centered school will systematically identify students in need of additional time and support and provide targeted interventions. In a PRTI, Tier 2 interventions are

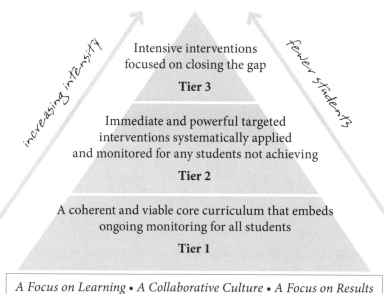

Figure 7-1: The pyramid response to intervention model

considered *supplemental*; the school's core instruction is assumed to be effective for most students (see Figure 7-1).

Because students struggle at school due to a variety of causes, including student effort, Tier 2 interventions must be designed to meet the needs of both failed learners (students who failed to learn) and intentional nonlearners (students who failed to try). Their needs are markedly different. A successful Tier 1 program should meet the needs of at least 75% of the student body, and an effective Tier 2 supplemental level will meet the needs of at least 15% more.

Support Intentional Nonlearners

An intentional nonlearner has chosen to opt out of learning. The problem is not that the initial instruction was not appropriate or effective for this student; rather, he or she did not demonstrate the desire or effort necessary to master the new skills or material. Intentional nonlearners are neither motivated by grades nor aware of the long-term implications for failing in school. They simply resist doing what they don't want to do.

In a traditional school, one that believes its mission is to provide students with the *opportunity* to learn, intentional nonlearners are left to suffer the consequences of their choices. A PLC school designs supplemental interventions that require intentional nonlearners to make the effort necessary to ensure success. Potential interventions for these students include:

- Mandatory study hall
- Mandatory homework help
- Frequent progress reports
- Study-skills classes
- Goal-setting and career planning support
- Targeted rewards

Mandatory Study Hall

Mandatory study hall provides intentional nonlearners with a quiet, structured environment in which they are required to complete their homework, classwork, or make-up assignments. Because the targeted students are capable of doing the work, a credentialed teacher is not necessarily needed to teach study hall, which may be supervised by school support staff or administration. Educators can schedule mandatory study hall sessions before or after school, at lunchtime, during recess, or as an assigned class.

Mandatory Homework Help

Like study hall, mandatory homework help sessions provide students with a structured environment to complete assignments, but homework help sessions go further to also offer academic assistance. Because homework help includes tutoring, a credentialed teacher is the best person to supervise this activity, although qualified support staff, peer tutors, and community volunteers may also be used. As with mandatory study hall, schools can schedule such assistance before, during, or after school.

Frequent Progress Reports

Because intentional nonlearners have an aversion to doing work, they often fall behind in their coursework very quickly. Teachers can find it an uphill battle to help these students make up missing assignments *and* keep up with their current ones. Student progress reports provided at least once every 3 weeks can help struggling students—and their families—monitor their academic progress.

Study-Skills Class

Intentional nonlearners also often fall behind because they lack organization skills for keeping track of assignments, budgeting time well, and submitting completed work on time or at all. To address this concern, teachers can assign students to a study-skills class, where organization and study skills can be taught and practiced daily.

Goal-Setting and Career Planning Support

As noted earlier, intentional nonlearners rarely understand the direct connection between their immediate performance in school and their future opportunities in life. This lack of awareness is usually due to their lack of maturity and life experience, as well as the tendency for underachieving students to have parents who did not successfully navigate their own schooling. To help address this problem, the school can provide students with opportunities to explore career options, set career goals, learn about the steps necessary to achieve them, and create an achievement plan. This planning can be introduced in the upper elementary grades, with an increased focus throughout junior and senior high school. Such efforts will add real-life relevance to learning, helping children make vital connections between the school's expectations today and their personal dreams for tomorrow.

Targeted Rewards

When trying to motivate students who show a lack of effort, many educators focus solely on punitive methods. Although such approaches sometimes are needed, teachers should more often reinforce positive student actions.

Many schools have difficulties with intentional nonlearners primarily because they allow their students the option of not learning in the first place. The bottom line in creating effective responses to such students is this: The school's desire for these learners to do the work must be significantly greater than the children's desire not to do it. If a school has the same "zero-tolerance" approach to lack of student effort as it does for drugs or violence, then it will become a "laziness-free" zone.

Support Failed Learners

In contrast to intentional nonlearners, failed learners have attempted to learn but have yet to demonstrate proficiency. The problem is not that they won't do the work, but that they don't know how. Whereas an intentional nonlearner's lack of success comes from his or her lack of effort, a failed learner's difficulties stem primarily from the school's inability to provide effective instruction to meet his or her educational needs. To understand why, consider again our formula for learning:

$$\textbf{Targeted Instruction } + \textbf{ Time } = \textbf{ Learning}$$

Targeted, Differentiated Instruction

Some failed learners don't benefit from initial instruction because the teacher's pedagogic practices did not correspond with the student's learning style. For example, when studying algebra, some students have difficulty understanding abstract concepts that are presented in a traditional lecture format. These students can learn abstract ideas, but the concepts must be taught in a more visual or tactile format to make the material more concrete. In general, until a teacher communicates new concepts in a way that a student who is struggling can understand, no amount of additional time or practice will help.

Additional Time

For other failed learners, the initial instruction of a new concept is adequate for them to begin to understand it, but they need additional time to master it. For example, a golf player who is learning a new swing from his coach might conceptually understand it but still require additional practice time and reinforcement to use the technique effectively during matches. Similarly, educators who provide students with opportunities for guided and independent practice help them to develop competency, gain confidence, and transfer learned concepts from short- to long-term memory. Of course, the amount of practice a particular student needs varies according to his or her prior knowledge, aptitude for the subject, learning style, and self-confidence.

Prerequisite Skill Review

Finally, some failed learners struggle with new content because they lack critical prerequisite skills and knowledge needed to truly grasp it. For example, third-grade students must first have mastered basic multiplication skills to learn long division. For students lacking such skills, supplemental interventions that solely provide them with additional practice in long division will prove useless. Instead, these students need a targeted intervention that addresses their learning gap—the basic skill of how to multiply.

To help with this type of need, the best "intervention" is prevention. Traditionally, most schools assign interventions for struggling students *after* they have had difficulties in their initial instruction. Yet a more effective strategy is to provide such learners a targeted review of the prerequisite skills *before* asking them to learn new concepts.

For example, before teaching their students how to write a Response to Literature essay, an eighth-grade language arts team determined that the children first needed to learn two critical prerequisite skills: the ability to understand *plot* and *foreshadowing*. Two weeks before starting their Response to Literature unit, the team created a preassessment on these concepts and then provided targeted interventions to students who did not demonstrate understanding.

Due to these preventive steps, the teachers' initial instruction on Response to Literature became significantly more effective. Had the team waited until after the initial instruction to address the needs of students with learning gaps, they would have had to teach the prerequisite concepts, reteach the new material, and address the failing students' lack of confidence.

This "preventive intervention" approach also can be extremely effective when teachers work with students whose native language is not English. Often, English-language learners struggle with core instruction because they lack proficiency in the academic vocabulary of the material. When teachers identify this vocabulary and preview it with students before initial instruction, non-native speakers have a greater chance of benefiting from the Tier 1 instruction.

Sometimes it is difficult to determine if a student is a failed learner or an intentional nonlearner. Failed learners who have struggled in school for a long time tend to give up trying. To a teacher new to this student, the child's lack of effort appears to show traits of an intentional nonlearner. Additionally, it is possible for a student to be an intentional nonlearner in one subject and a failed learner in another. The purpose of these terms is not to label students, but to clarify two causes that require markedly different solutions.

Targeting Interventions

Given the many reasons why students fail to learn, a PRTI must design a variety of supplemental interventions to meet diverse needs. The more targeted each intervention is, the more effective it will be. Students should be grouped for intervention by the cause of their difficulties, rather than by the symptoms. For example, a traditional school may group kids for an intervention because they all scored below proficient on the grade-level math assessment. But failure on this test is the *symptom* of learning difficulties. The real question is, what is the cause—for each student? For students who failed due to lack of effort, a PRTI will provide an intervention designed to support their study skills. For those who failed due to gaps in their prior learning, a PRTI offers a different intervention to teach the prior knowledge they need.

Unfortunately, most schools tend to offer broad interventions that do not meet any particular learning need. For example, schools commonly provide mandatory homework help to failing students, regardless of whether they are intentional nonlearners, have learning gaps, or need a different classroom instructional style. Given this wide variety of student needs, the supervising teacher is in a near-impossible position. The homework-help instructor cannot simultaneously teach prerequisite skills to students with learning gaps, reteach the initial instruction to children who need a different teaching style, and help motivate the intentional nonlearners.

And after once trying to bridge instruction among these very different types of students, teachers may never again volunteer to lead interventions! Without targeted programs designed to address specific student needs, both teacher and student are set up for failure.

Identify and Place Students

Clearly, an extremely effective student identification and placement procedure is absolutely essential to a pyramid response to intervention. If a school does not accurately identify every student in need of intervention, determine why each student is struggling, and place each student in the proper intervention, then all the school's efforts to design effective interventions will be rendered virtually useless. To be most successful, this process must also be frequent enough that students don't fall too far behind and flexible enough to adjust as student needs change. Finally, elementary and secondary schools have markedly different structures and different advantages and obstacles in referring students. The school must carefully design a system of decision protocols that will address the following elements of the identification process:

- Who needs to be part of the collaborative, problem-solving team that will identify students in need of additional time and support?

- How often will this team meet?

- What criteria and data will the team need to make informed, timely, and targeted decisions about each student?

- How will the team growth monitor each student's progress?

Elementary Level

Without question, the individuals best qualified to identify a particular student in need of interventions are those who work most directly with the student. At the elementary level, the most qualified staff will likely be the child's classroom teacher or a grade-level team of teachers, if they share students. For this reason, many elementary schools use grade-level team meetings to identify and place students in interventions. Because many under-represented students also work with a special education teacher or reading specialist, specialist staff members should be included in these grade-level meetings. Specialists also add instructional expertise in their area of focus, which is vital when designing and implementing highly effective, research-based interventions. Finally, frequent administrative participation in these meetings is critical to provide and coordinate resources. (This model can also work well for secondary schools in which students are assigned to interdisciplinary teams.) Because identification and placement decisions are based primarily on student assessment data, universal screening and progress-monitoring data are critical.

Secondary Level

In contrast, because secondary students often have five, six, or seven teachers, frequent grade-level meetings are an impractical way for second-ary schools to identify students at risk and place them into interventions. Nevertheless, systematic input from all of a student's teachers is critical. For this reason, most secondary schools require every teacher to refer stu-dents for additional support and compile these referrals to create a com-plete picture of each student's needs. Administrative and/or counseling staff can serve as intervention coordinators and use this combined student information to place students into interventions.

For this type of system to work best, each teacher must provide the intervention coordinator with not only grades and assessment data, but also his or her sense as to why the student is struggling in class. Without this level of information, the coordinator will not know whether the referred student is an intentional nonlearner or failed learner and thus may choose the wrong kind of interventions.

Tier 2 in Elementary Schools

Marjorie Veeh Elementary School in Tustin, California, is a K–5 school that sits on the outskirts of a large urban area and primarily serves socioeconomically disadvantaged English-language learners. To meet the main population's language needs, the school's core program focuses on reading and writing.

During weekly collaborative meetings, grade-level teams identify essential learning standards, prerequisite skills, and academic vocabulary needed to learn the new material, as well as the formative assessments that will be used to measure student learning throughout the units of study.

Additionally, each grade-level team meets every other week with the principal, reading specialist, and special education teachers to review student common assessment data, design interventions, identify students in need of supplemental support, and place students in the proper intervention. Once a child is placed in an intervention, the team will monitor each student's progress and make adjustments as needed.

Because the staff at Marjorie Veeh recognizes that most of their students need supplemental English language instruction to access the core curriculum, every day each grade level preteaches the upcoming unit's essential academic vocabulary in flexible groups based upon each student's level of English proficiency.

To provide additional time and targeted instruction to failed learners, twice a week each grade-level team can pull targeted groups of students from physical education for additional practice or different instructional techniques to learn essential standards. Additionally, while all students participate each morning in 2 hours of uninterrupted, grade-level language arts instruction, the school's reading specialist works with each grade-level team to identify students with learning gaps and pulls specific students for supplemental support during afternoon enrichment activities.

For intentional nonlearners, the school started an after-school homework club called the Learning Center. Students assigned to the Learning Center receive highly structured homework help for 2 hours after school every day. On Fridays, students who satisfactorily complete their assignments for the week earn the privilege of participating in "Fun Friday" activities, which include games, sports, and art activities. These targeted, timely supplemental interventions have proven to be very effective for the students and staff at Marjorie Veeh. Over a 3-year period, Veeh's average yearly progress (AYP) proficiency rate rose 43% in language arts and 50% in math.

Tier 2 in Secondary Schools

At Pioneer Middle School in Tustin, California, the school year begins with a universal screening of every student in reading, writing, and mathematics. Using the results, the counseling staff works with department teams to reconsider the current instructional program for students who demonstrated significant concerns in any of these core learning areas. Options include academic support electives in reading, language arts, English language development, and mathematics. Subsequently, every 3 weeks, teachers recommend their students with an overall grade below 75% to the grade-level coordinators of the school's intervention program. Educators make referrals electronically, utilizing the school's student data-management software. As part of the referral process, teachers provide the intervention coordinator with each student's current grade and information about his or her work habits and citizenship; they also use comment codes to indicate whether the student is an intentional nonlearner (such as "late or missing work") or a failed learner ("difficulty understanding concepts").

After a designated staff member compiles teacher referrals, the school assigns an intervention coordinator to each referred student. Based upon the child's needs, the coordinator can assign him or her to one or both of the following:

- *Mandatory tutorial*—This daily tutorial period provides teachers with extended time to reteach essential concepts. Referred students attend in one or more areas of need, based on teacher recommendations.

- *Mandatory homework help*—The student goes to daily lunchtime and/or after-school homework help sessions.

The school has committed itself to contacting the parents and guardians of children referred for intervention and providing them with a report every 3 weeks of the children's current progress, the school's areas of concern, and the interventions that the school will provide. After 3 weeks, teachers can again refer students to interventions, based on their updated grades. From this information, the intervention coordinator determines whether to promote students from the intervention program, maintain them at their current level of support, or provide them with more intensive interventions. This process ensures timely progress monitoring of students in the intervention program.

What If Tier 2 Interventions Are Not Working?

Obviously, the goal of Tier 2 interventions is to provide targeted students with the additional time and support they need to succeed in the school's Tier 1 program. As student progress is monitored to determine the effectiveness of the interventions, some students will need a greater intensity of support to achieve. This increased intensity could include more frequent application of the Tier 2 interventions. When a child does not respond at all to the Tier 2 interventions, however, he or she may need the interventions provided at Tier 3, including, in some cases, an entirely new core program.

What are your Tier 2 supplemental interventions?

See page 189 for an activity to help your leadership team evaluate your Tier 2 program. Discuss each element that should be found in a Tier 2 program, and honestly record your current reality. Next, record your long-term desired outcome, and establish a few short-term goals.

Visit **go.solution-tree.com/rti**
to download this activity.

Chapter Eight
Tier 3:
The Intensive Level

What RTI does is put everybody on the same playing field. It doesn't matter what your language structure is, whether or not you're disabled, or whether or not you're poor. What matters is what you need to progress at a satisfactory pace in the general curriculum.

—Wayne Sailor, associate director, Beach Center on Families and Disability, University of Kansas

*M*any students receiving supplemental Tier 2 interventions at Forest Glenn Elementary School seemed to be making good progress. In fact, several students had made such good progress that the SST deemed the interventions no longer necessary to their educational progress. A few students had not made enough progress to leave Tier 2, however, and a few others had not grown at all, according to the results from progress monitoring. The SST studied the progress-monitoring data carefully and subsequently decided to administer even more intensive interventions to the students who had not responded sufficiently to Tier 2 interventions.

At Forest Glenn, Tier 3 interventions are delivered more frequently than Tier 2 interventions: as often as every day for up to 60 minutes in addition to the core curriculum. The SST recommended a 16-week "dose" of Tier 3 interventions for these students who needed intensive support with decoding and vocabulary development. During this 16-week treatment, interventionists monitored the progress of the students twice weekly, using running records to record words read correctly in a standardized period of time and plotting the results to check the trend for each student. Were students catching up or falling further behind their grade-level peers?

When the SST met several months later to examine the data, they used their decision protocols to interpret the data in a systematic, consistent way. Some students were returned to Tier 2 as they had almost caught up with their classmates and with some continued, albeit less intensive, interventions, would soon do so. Other students seemed to be responding to the Tier 3 interventions, but not quickly enough to catch up with their classmates, so the SST ordered another 16 weeks of the interventions that seemed to be helping these students make significant progress.

However, the responses of two of the students, David and Maria, were especially disappointing. Despite the intensity of the Tier 3 interventions they had received, David and Maria showed almost no growth whatsoever. Progress-monitoring data clearly indicated that they were not responding to the interventions. The SST team realized that David and Maria might need the additional support offered by special education through the IEP process.

Using the Right Intensive Interventions at the Right Time

Some students who have received Tier 1 core instruction and Tier 2 supplemental interventions will continue to have difficulty learning (see Figure 8-1, page 101). They need instruction that is even more explicit and intensive, and even more targeted and tailored to their individual needs. Interventions that provide such instruction are known as *Tier 3 or intensive. Intensive* refers to the amount of time per day, the number of days per week, the number of weeks of instruction, and the number of students receiving the intervention at a given time. Tier 3 interventions generally last 12–18 weeks, and usually serve no more than 5–10% of the student population.

Tier 3 interventions are designed for students who show low content-area skills and/or lack of progress over time when provided with Tier 1

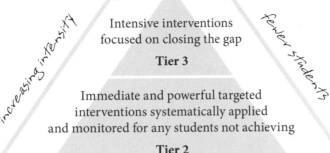

increasing intensity

fewer students

Intensive interventions
focused on closing the gap

Tier 3

Immediate and powerful targeted
interventions systematically applied
and monitored for any students not achieving

Tier 2

A coherent and viable core curriculum that embeds
ongoing monitoring for all students

Tier 1

A Focus on Learning • A Collaborative Culture • A Focus on Results

Figure 8-1: The pyramid response to intervention model

and Tier 2 interventions. Tier 3 interventions, especially in reading for grades K–3, are typically conducted one on one, or with no more than a 3:1 student-teacher ratio. Upper-grade elementary and secondary schools should aspire toward this kind of ratio, but it may not be practical for many schools. Tier 3 interventions are targeted to address very specific areas of deficiency for individual students. The main differences between Tiers 2 and 3 are not necessarily the interventions themselves, but the frequency, duration, and progress-monitoring requirements. For example, Tier 3 interventions might be delivered for at least 1 hour per day (or two half-hour sessions per day), while student progress is monitored at least twice each week. Many schools have strategically reworked the master schedule or utilized existing personnel in new and creative ways to provide Tier 3 interventions that are guided, but not necessarily delivered exclusively, by the classroom teacher.

Like Tier 2 interventions, Tier 3 interventions should be mandatory, not invitational, and provided during the regular school day, not before or after school. As Sharon Vaughn and Greg Roberts (2007) state, these interventions should "be intensive enough to provide students with a reasonable opportunity to 'catch up' to grade-level expectations. Students should not be 'locked into' the intervention for long periods of time without ongoing progress monitoring and consideration of their trajectory for meeting grade-level expectations" (p. 44).

Sometimes teachers can adapt Tier 2 interventions for use at Tier 3 by increasing their frequency and duration. At the intensive level, many children require daily interventions of an hour or more. Staff should monitor their progress at least twice each week to see if the "prescription" is working. Since students at Tier 3 have not responded sufficiently to previous supplemental interventions, frequent progress monitoring is especially important to establish that a student's lack of success was not caused by a lack of either effective instruction or systematic and intensive interventions, which would indicate the possible existence of a specific learning disability.

Table 8-1 provides an overview of how Tier 3 interventions in reading might be defined compared to those in Tiers 1 and 2.

Table 8-1: Tiered Reading Interventions

	Tier 1	Tier 2	Tier 3
Definition	Reading instruction and programs, including ongoing professional development and benchmark assessments (3 times per year)	Instructional intervention employed to supplement, enhance, and support Tier 1; takes place in small groups	Individualized reading instruction extended beyond the time allocated for Tier 1; groups of 1–3 students
Focus	All students	Students identified with reading difficulties who have not responded to Tier 1 efforts	Students with marked difficulties in reading or reading disabilities who have not adequately responded to Tier 1 and Tier 2 efforts
Program	Scientifically based reading instruction and curriculum emphasizing the critical elements	Specialized, scientifically based reading instruction and curriculum emphasizing the critical elements	Sustained, intensive, scientifically based reading instruction and curriculum highly responsive to students' needs
Instruction	Sufficient opportunities to practice throughout the school day	• Additional attention, focus, support • Additional opportunities to practice embedded throughout the day • Preteach, review skills; frequent opportunities to practice skills	Carefully designed and implemented, explicit, systematic instruction

Table continues on page 103→

	Tier 1	Tier 2	Tier 3
Interventionist	General education teacher	Personnel determined by the school (classroom teacher, specialized reading teacher, other trained personnel)	Personnel determined by the school (such as the specialized reading teacher or special education teacher)
Setting	General education classroom	Appropriate setting designated by the school	Appropriate setting designated by the school
Grouping	Flexible grouping	Homogeneous small-group instruction (with teacher-student ratios of 1:4 or 1:5)	Homogeneous small-group instruction (with teacher-student ratios of 1:1 or 1:2)
Time	Minimum of 90 minutes per day	20–30 minutes per day in addition to Tier 1	50-minute sessions (or longer) per day depending upon appropriateness of Tier 1
Assessment	Benchmark assessments at beginning, middle, and end of academic year	Progress monitoring twice a month on target skill to ensure adequate progress and learning	Progress monitoring more than twice a month on target skill to ensure adequate progress learning

Adapted from Vaughn Gross Center for Reading and Language Arts (2005)

Educators shouldn't automatically identify students who don't respond to Tier 3 interventions as candidates for special education. Rather, in such cases, educators should convene Student Study Team meeting to evaluate whether the interventions are being delivered with fidelity and whether they are the right prescriptions based upon the student's "learning diagnosis."

Schools should view intensive interventions as supplemental to core instruction, and classroom teachers should continue to provide the same guaranteed, viable curriculum to these students and to others who aren't receiving intensive interventions. However, when diagnostic evidence suggests that the student requires a radically redesigned curriculum that will accelerate learning to the point that the student can be returned to the core curriculum, intensive interventions may supplant the core curriculum.

When schools have strengthened their core curriculum, trained teachers to differentiate that curriculum, and then provided targeted supplemental interventions at Tier 2 with fidelity, more of the same might not be the best prescription. However, when students are receiving Tier 3 interventions that supplement rather than supplant the core curriculum, classroom teachers should continue to intervene with students as part of regular classroom instruction.

The FCRR: A Source for Tier 3 Interventions

As educators build and refine a pyramid response to intervention, they often ask where they can find listings of research-based interventions that can truly meet the needs of Tier 3 students. The Florida Center for Reading Research (FCRR) is one of the best sources for such information. When staff decides that a student is not responding to core programs, they can use the quite specific, focused programs that FCRR has reviewed (see Table 8-2) and that provide systematic and explicit instruction in components of reading skills.

Table 8-2: FCRR-Reviewed Tier 3 Interventions

Program Name	Group Size	Length of Daily Lesson
Corrective Reading	4–5 students or whole group	45 minutes
Failure Free Reading	1–1 or small groups	45–60 minutes
Kaleidoscope	Whole group and small group	120 minutes
Language!	Small groups	90 minutes
Spell, Read, P.A.T.	3–5 students	60–90 minutes
Success for All	Small groups	90 minutes
Wilson Reading System	Whole group and small group	55–90 minutes
Voyager Passport	3–6 students	40 minutes

FCRR-Reviewed Programs for Students with Reading Deficiencies

Phonics and Phonemic Awareness

- Earobics (predominantly computer-based)
- Phono-Graphix
- Read, Write, and Type (computer-based)

Fluency

- Great Leaps
- QuickReads
- Read Naturally (computer-based)
- Soliloquy Reading Assistant (computer-based)

Word Analysis, Language, and Vocabulary

- Elements of Reading: Vocabulary
- QuickReads
- Rewards

Reading Comprehension

- Project CRISS
- QuickReads
- Soar to Success

Tier 3 in Elementary Schools
(Adapted from National Research Center on Learning Disabilities, 2006b)

Rosewood Elementary School in Vero Beach, Florida, enrolls approximately 550 students in grades K–5, with four or five classrooms per grade level. Approximately 30% of the students receive free or reduced-price lunches. Many of the school's students experience reading difficulties.

In Tier 1, students receive a research-based core curriculum to ensure they have the best possible chance to be successful in meeting grade-level standards. Rosewood's supplemental Tier 2 interventions are designed for students who need more time and support in reaching grade-level standards. These are delivered along with Tier 1 interventions, but classroom teachers work with smaller groups to increase the intensity of the interventions.

A large cross-section of Rosewood's staff is involved in delivering Tier 3 interventions, including the general education teacher, reading coach, student support specialist, elementary specialist, school psychologist, ESL teacher, and speech-language pathologist. These intensive interventions are delivered in the regular classroom and may consist of an additional 2 hours a day, 5 days a week of targeted instruction. Rosewood's Tier 3 interventions are usually delivered one-on-one, but never to groups larger than five. Interventions at Tier 3 include the Harcourt Trophies Intervention Program with the American Federation of Teachers' Educational Research and Dissemination "Five-Step Plan," Earobics, Road to the Code, Great Leaps, and QuickReads. Individual interventions are used to address specific areas of concern. School staff monitor progress weekly using DIBELS, AIMSweb Oral Reading Fluency, or AIMSweb Maze.

Tier 3 in High Schools
(Adapted from Duffy, 2006)

The Long Beach Unified School District in California uses frequent progress monitoring and tiered interventions in order to meet the needs of all students in its regular education programs. In the spring, all eighth-grade middle school students receive universal screening to determine which students will need more time and support. The screening examines several measures of student achievement, including the California standards test, student course grades, and an assessment that is part of the *Language!* curriculum the district has adopted. In the fall, the district administers a battery of eighth-grade assessments to its entering ninth-grade high school students. While all incoming students receive core literacy instruction, students entering high school who are a half year to 2 years behind standards are also enrolled in a literacy course that provides them with additional time and support in addition to the core literacy instruction.

Entering high school students who are more than 2 years below grade level receive intensive support through a double-block language arts program. For this intensive language support program, Long Beach Unified uses the Lindamood-Bell curriculum, which helps students who have reading difficulties by focusing on developing their phonemic skills.

In addition, *Language!* is also used for intensive instructional programs in literacy. Typically, students spend a semester in Lindamood-Bell before transitioning into *Language!* Teachers use tests taken from the Lindamood-Bell and *Language!* curricula as progress-monitoring tools for these students receiving Tier 3 interventions.

In addition to this systematic approach to providing more time and support for students, Long Beach Unified also provides support for teachers, through regular meetings, summer institutes, and instructional coaches who provide job-embedded training. While this approach shares certain key characteristics with RTI, Long Beach educators do not call its approach RTI, but rather "best practice for all students." Staff ask, "What do we want all students to learn? How will we know if they've learned? How will we respond when some students don't learn?"

According to Judy Elliot, former assistant superintendent at the district's Office of Special Education, Long Beach educators base decisions on multiple data points. Long Beach views this diagnostic and prescriptive approach as good instruction for all students rather than as a process to diagnose students with learning disabilities. Their approach has been so successful at the high school level that the district has recently applied it to middle schools. As a result, roughly 7% of students in Long Beach have IEPs, as opposed to an average of 12–14% nationally.

What are your Tier 3 intensive interventions?

See page 190 for an activity to help your leadership team evaluate your Tier 3 program. Discuss each element that should be found in a Tier 3 program, and honestly record your current reality. Next, record your long-term desired outcome, and establish a few short-term goals.

Visit **go.solution-tree.com/rti**
to download this activity.

Chapter Nine

The Role of Behavioral Interventions

I've come to the frightening conclusion that I am the decisive element in the classroom. It's my personal approach that creates the climate. It's my daily mood that makes the weather. As a teacher I possess a tremendous power to make a child's life miserable or joyous. I can be a tool of torture or an instrument of inspiration. I can humiliate or humor, hurt or heal. In all situations, it is my response that decides whether a crisis will be escalated or de-escalated, and a child humanized or dehumanized.

—Haim Ginott, Clinical Psychologist and Author

Tina was a seventh-grade student whose impulsive behavior created many problems throughout the day. In the classroom, Tina had difficulty keeping comments to herself, while with her classmates, Tina had difficulty reading their social clues. Other students didn't include her in their social groups, and Tina didn't understand why others didn't like her. As the school year progressed, one of Tina's teachers, Bill Morrison, felt a parent-teacher conference was necessary.

"Tina is bright," Bill told her parents, "but her behavior is having a negative impact on her learning as well as her social development."

Tina's parents looked at each other and sighed. They were not surprised; they had heard this information from Tina's previous teachers. At the end of the meeting, Bill felt that not much had been accomplished by this latest telling of apparently old news.

So Bill met with the school's student study team, comprised of the school counselor, school psychologist, and the principal. He described Tina's behaviors in class and summarized the parent conference. The SST concluded that a functional behavioral analysis (FBA) was needed; they hypothesized that the motivation behind Tina's behaviors was attention. If the FBA confirmed the team's hypothesis, the team would then brainstorm interventions that would include understanding the antecedents to Tina's outbursts and teaching her new skills and consequences for her behavior.

After observing Tina during different parts of the school day and meeting with Tina's other teachers, the school psychologist, Roberta, called another meeting of the SST.

"These problem behaviors have been occurring for at least the last 2 school years," Roberta reminded the group, "but actually, no formal interventions have ever been implemented. Everyone has talked about Tina's problem, but I'm not sure that anything has been done to help her." Tina's parents had conceded to Roberta that these behaviors also happened in other settings, during family events, and even at church.

In order to minimize the amount of negative attention Tina received, the SST came up with an intervention plan that included removing Tina from settings that seemed to precede the problem behavior as well as providing her with positive support peers throughout the day. In order to teach Tina new skills, the counselor agreed to meet with her individually and in a small group to make her more aware of the problem behaviors and teach her replacement behaviors. The SST agreed to meet again in 2 weeks to assess the effectiveness of the plan.

Two weeks later, as a result of everyone's efforts, Tina had become much more aware of her negative behaviors—especially when asked to self-monitor her own blurt-outs. Overall, the team was very pleased with the sharp decrease in negative behaviors, but agreed to reconvene again in 2 months to assess the continued results of the plan.

When the team met again 2 months later, Tina's behavior had continued to improve. Knowing that changes in social behavior can be more difficult to sustain, the SST decided to continue with the plan and to meet again at the end of the year to review the plan and make recommendations for the following school year.

Behavior and Academic Achievement

Behavior and academic achievement are inextricably linked. A student's academic success in school is directly related to the student's attention, engagement, and behavior. The higher the expectations for scholarly behaviors and the better the supports for students experiencing difficulties—whether mild, moderate, or severe—the more academic success can be achieved. In fact, one study (Hawkins, Catalano, Kosterman, Abbott, & Hill, 1999), found that when schools raised their level of academic achievement, behavior problems decreased—and when schools worked to decrease behavior problems, academic achievement improved.

In some situations it is difficult to distinguish which problem came first, the academic or behavioral difficulty—whether the child "can't do it" or "won't do it." In earlier chapters, we made the case for examining data in order to make important decisions about students and their learning as part of PRTI; this kind of data-driven decision-making should not be done in isolation by individual teachers, but by teams working together to understand what is working and what is not. Dealing with student behavior is no exception. Many of the same principles that apply to PRTI in academic areas apply to behavior as well. Schools that intervene early and successfully will set high expectations, explicitly teach students how to behave, gather data to inform decisions, and modify schoolwide and student-specific programs based on a diagnosis of needs.

As we have seen, in a PRTI, students who experience difficulty in learning are provided with a specific level of instruction and intervention in an academic area, and then are frequently assessed while continuing to receive support that is either modified or intensified based upon their response to intervention. PRTI addresses student behavior in the same proactive way. Instead of "waiting for students to fail" as in traditional discipline programs, PRTI teaches all students the expected behaviors as part of the core behavioral curriculum. Behaviors are frequently assessed, and students are consistently recognized and rewarded when they display those behaviors. When they don't, they are provided with scientifically validated interventions and increasing time and support until they achieve success.

Using a unified, systematic approach to examine all kinds of data helps teams to unravel the relationship between behavior and academic performance. Why wouldn't teachers want to examine such data as referrals, suspensions, and expulsions in order to learn how to better support their students? If it is important to learn which students are under-represented academically in order to provide them with additional time and support, wouldn't it be equally important to identify which students need more attention and support regarding their behavior?

Frank Gresham (2004) described four major components of behavorial interventions in RTI. According to Gresham:

1. *Academic and behavioral interventions are based upon the severity of the problem.* RTI's three-tiered approach is entirely consistent with this thought, as at each subsequent tier, fewer students with more intense problems receive increasingly intensive levels of time and support.

2. *Students' responses to intervention provide the basis for changing, modifying, or intensifying interventions.* Systematically collected behavioral data (such as office referrals) provide the basis for making adjustments and decisions to behavioral interventions.

3. *Evidence-based practices are used:*

   • To select interventions

   • To evaluate the effectiveness of the interventions themselves

   • To assess the degree of fidelity with which interventions have been administered

4. *Social validation is the final component of implementing behavioral interventions through RTI.* At the end of each intervention cycle, we should ask all those affected by the student(s) if the approaches used and the results obtained are consistent with their values and the culture of the school.

It should be noted that Gresham's third component is entirely consistent with the third "big idea" of the PLC: a focus on results. DuFour, DuFour, & Eaker (2008, p. 469) define *results orientation* as "a focus on outcomes rather than inputs or intentions. In PLCs, members are committed to achieving desired results and are hungry for evidence that their efforts are producing the intended outcomes."

A school that successfully promotes positive behaviors understands that learning and behavior are mutually supportive. Appropriate behaviors create environments in which learning can most productively occur; students whose needs are supported and who experience academic success are less likely to act out. Schools employing strategies supported by the research of Sugai and Horner (2006) have long viewed student behaviors within a pyramid, with approximately 80% of students consistently behaving appropriately, 15% of students requiring a moderate amount of redirection and behavior remediation, and 5% of students requiring individualized behavior plans. These strategies have been known as *effective behavior supports* (EBS), and are now known as *positive behavior support* (PBS) or *positive behavioral interventions and supports* (PBIS).

The U.S. Office of Special Education has established the National Technical Assistance Center to disseminate information and research on PBIS. The PBIS website (www.pbis.org) provides information and technical support about behavioral systems that may help inform schools attempting to build a pyramid response to intervention. Figure 9-1 shows the relationship between the two kinds of interventions.

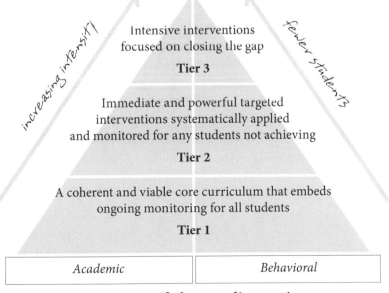

Figure 9-1: A unified system of interventions.

PBIS strategies are employed by thousands of schools in over 30 states nationwide (U.S. Office of Special Education, 2008). As schools study the language in IDEIA 2004, they are increasingly adopting the logic of RTI to organize and deliver both academic and behavioral support for all students (Cook & Sprague, 2008). The PBIS website provides rich resources to schools attempting to include both behavior and academics as part of their overall intervention program—including links to other behavioral intervention models, such as the work being conducted at the Behavior and Reading Improvement Center at the University of North Carolina at Charlotte.

To reinforce the logical connections between academics and behavior in RTI, IDEIA provides guidelines for responding when a child's behavior impedes the child's learning or that of others: Conduct a functional behavior assessment (FBA), and develop a positive behavior support plan. A positive behavior support plan specifies what the *adults* will do to address such challenging behavior and includes "proactive action planning to address behavior(s) that are impeding learning" and "positive behavioral interventions, strategies and supports" (IDEIA Section 614(d)(2)(B)).

As Diana Browning Wright and her coauthors (2007) note, "Behavior Support Plans should focus on understanding 'why' the behavior occurred (i.e. 'the function' or 'communicative intent') then focus on teaching an alternative behavior that meets the student's need in a more acceptable way. This includes making instructional and environmental changes, providing reinforcement, reactive strategies and effective communication" (p. 6). Accordingly, a PRTI includes a three-tiered continuum of behavioral interventions that, as with academic interventions, increase in intensity: Tier 1 focuses on preventing the development of problem behavior while Tiers 2 and 3 strive to reduce its impact or intensity. A three-tiered model has been implemented successfully in Oregon as the Effective Behavior and Instructional Support system (Sadler & Zinn, 2005). Like the academic models discussed in earlier chapters, this model requires periodic universal screening of students. Teacher teams examine a standard set of data and sort students into groups that are provided with increasingly intensive interventions depending on their behavior and responses to intervention. Movement through the tiers is a dynamic process, with students entering and exiting according to their progress-monitoring data.

Supporting Positive Student Behavior

The first steps in establishing a climate that supports positive behavior and high levels of learning are: 1) Identify the 6–10 key areas in which it is important or necessary to focus staff and student attention (past data or focus groups may help identify these areas), 2) demonstrate and model positive behaviors to students, and 3) monitor for adherence to the rules that have been communicated. The precise behaviors that are desired in each of these key areas must be articulated, written, and communicated to the staff and school community.

Identify and Model Positive Behaviors

In the same way that teacher teams answer the question, "What is it we want all kids to learn?" so should they ask and answer the questions, "How do we want all students to behave?" and "What behaviors are we trying to prevent?" Schools can teach and reward students for complying with a relatively small set of basic rules that can be translated into more specific expectations depending upon the setting. For example, a basic rule such as "be safe" might be translated into specific expectations that differ according to various locations—the library, the playground, the lunch room, or the parking lot.

It is also critical to explicitly show students what good behavior looks like. Many schools choose to devote a half-day, sometimes twice a year, to demonstrating the types of behaviors the school values. For example, some schools set up stations around campus at key locations such as restrooms, the playground, or walkways. Teachers perform for groups of students that rotate from station to station, first demonstrating the wrong way to behave—which usually elicits laughs—then demonstrating the correct way to behave. Students from the audience may assist to create further engagement. These demonstrations are very explicit, and the correct behaviors are consistently reinforced in the days, weeks, and months that follow. Involving and communicating with students is crucial. Many schools employing PBIS strategies create mottos that reflect their behavioral expectations, such as "Show respect, make good choices, and solve your problems" or "Respect, responsibility, and readiness." If we expect students to act responsibly, we must teach them how to control their own behavior.

Gather Data on Adherence

In a behavior management system that follows the tenets of PRTI, data becomes more important than ever before. In the old paradigm, written referrals for inappropriate behavior were sent to the office for only the most serious offenses. In a PRTI behavior support system, *all* misbehaviors are identified, reported, recorded, and analyzed; students are held accountable for high expectations in behavior as well as academics. A more comprehensive, detailed referral is necessary, one that provides information such as:

- Student name

- Staff member who reported the offense

- When and where the offense occurred (for example, the classroom, restroom, cafeteria)

- The nature and degree of the offense (for example, aggressive physical contact, harassment, minor class disruption)

- Others involved in the incident

- Possible motivation for the offense

- Follow-up actions (for example, detention, parent contact, suspension, warning)

Data warehousing and mining software, some of it quite inexpensive, can provide progress-monitoring reports. This will allow schools to make changes to supervision schedules (if, for example, afternoon recess has many more referrals than morning recess) or provide the information needed to retrain or remind students. These reports can also be used in parent conferences and communications.

In a PRTI system, more data is collected, and it is collected in a standardized way across the campus. The key to the success of the entire endeavor is recognizing positive behaviors far more often than negative behaviors. We recommend a minimum 5:1 ratio. A system of schoolwide rewards is helpful; incentive cards or something similarly cheap can be freely distributed to students behaving appropriately. When students accumulate a given number of these incentives, depending on their grade level, they may be acknowledged by the principal by being allowed to select a gift from a "treasure box" in the office, given a special certificate in front of their classes, or given extended lunch, parking permits, or off-campus privileges. Beginning with Adlai Stevenson High School, some PLC sites have been very effective at identifying things that truly motivate students and using them to reward positive student behavior. In a PRTI, positive behaviors are constantly reinforced, and all students are provided the opportunity to "win."

Tier 1 Interventions

The purpose of Tier 1 behavioral intervention is prevention: to provide a positive environment for *all* students through the use of effective classroom management along with differentiated instruction.

An efficient, orderly classroom, in which students feel safe to take risks and learning time is optimized, involves more than discipline plans, punishments, and rules. Classrooms that maximize instructional time provide students with predictable structures and are ultraorganized. Teachers in these classrooms take the time at the beginning of the year to "train" students on the procedures for learning; they consistently model and demonstrate the appropriate academic behaviors in the classroom, and they expect high levels of engagement from all students at all times. Effective classroom management practices are fundamental Tier 1 components of a PRTI system.

Rather than simply issuing a set of rules and then punishing students who don't comply, schools should proactively teach all students how they are expected to behave and then reward them for following the rules. It is widely understood that the academic curriculum must contain the critical content and skills every student is expected to learn. Similarly, a behavioral curriculum should contain those social skills and behaviors that all students are expected to display. This universal curriculum should consist of schoolwide expectations, rules, and procedures, along with protocols that explain how to teach them to all students.

Fortunately, educators have moved beyond using punishment as a means to suppress behavior, or simply rewarding a student if he or she stops the problem behavior. Rather than waiting for students to misbehave and then punishing them (a behavioral wait-to-fail model), a proactive approach helps establish a condition in which appropriate behavior is the norm: a kind of behavioral core curriculum. By teaching and reinforcing the expected behaviors, teachers and other professionals increase the probability that the majority of students will act according to the expectations. This approach serves as a proactive intervention for students with a history of problem behavior (Sandomierski, Kincaid, & Algozzine, 2007). Approximately 80% of students should respond appropriately to this core level and receive only one, if any, referral during an entire year.

In the Tier 1 program, administrators should see every referral written and should follow up personally with each student for each transgression. These brief conservations should be positive reminders of the high expectations at the school. Part of the Tier 1 program should include reviewing the specific rules and expectations with *all* students when periodic reviews of behavioral data reveal that certain times of day or types of misbehavior have become an area of concern. These reviews may take place during brief assemblies or perhaps during a recess in an elementary school.

When this kind of universal approach to behavior intervention at Tier 1 is carried out with fidelity, schools can begin to identify students truly in need of additional support. One method used to identify these students is *multiple gating*, a series of increasingly precise assessments (Feil, Severson, & Walker, 2002). These assessments include broad teacher measures of all students, followed by more specific teacher ratings that record the frequency and intensity of the inappropriate behaviors, followed by direct observation of student behavior. Other methods used to identify students include Drummond's (1993) student risk screening scale, office discipline referral tracking, and *direct behavior ratings*, that is, "performance-based recording procedures used to collect teacher ratings of a student specific to a predetermined set of behaviors" (Chafouleas, Riley-Tilman, & Sugai, 2007, p. 540).

Students who continue to display inappropriate behaviors despite the proactive approaches employed at Tier 1 should receive interventions that are more targeted and individualized at Tier 2.

Tier 2 Interventions

While a preventative approach works for many students, some will not respond when we communicate what we expect them to do and try to motivate them to do it. However, when we promote positive behaviors by all students, we can reduce the number of *documented* behavior problems. This allows staff to focus on those students who truly need more support, rather than being overwhelmed by the sheer number of campuswide referrals. Support at Tier 2 for an additional 15–20% of students is more targeted, individualized, and intensive, provided to small groups of students on a weekly basis, often in the form of a social skills club, "check in/check out" with an adult, group counseling, mentoring programs, or an actual behavior plan.

These interventions should be relatively easy to administer to small groups of students and should not be overly burdensome to classroom teachers. Support from a counselor, psychologist, or other trained staff member can be scheduled during recess, lunch, before school, after school, or even during class time, if no other times are available. These small groups can focus on the specific issues that may be contributing to students' misbehaviors. Progress monitoring can be efficiently conducted at Tier 2 by using teacher rating scales to measure progress and provide specific feedback to the student. Samples of these scales can be found at the Florida PBS website (http://flpbs.fmhi.usf.edu). As with Tier 1 interventions, Tier 2 interventions must be carried out with fidelity before accurate decisions can be made to send students on to Tier 3 interventions or return them to the regular setting. This means that we need to not only evaluate a student's response to Tier 2 interventions, but also evaluate how well the interventions were delivered by staff.

Behavior data should be periodically reviewed and shared with all staff. This monthly (or weekly, if at all possible) review will identify students who have received the most number of referrals. The specifics of these students' difficulties can then be examined and a plan developed.

The classroom teacher can initiate a behavior contract that sets goals for specific types of behavior, with rewards to be earned immediately upon improvement. Parent conferences and more frequent home-to-school communication should also occur. Check-ins from administrators should occur more regularly.

Staff should be aware of who is in Tier 2 and their types of misbehaviors. When these students are in situations in which they have previously had difficulties and they behave appropriately, they should be immediately recognized and rewarded. However, when students fail to respond to Tier 2 interventions, schools need to have even more intensive and targeted behavioral interventions as part of PRTI.

Tier 3 Interventions

For a few students, even Tier 2's more targeted and focused support may not be enough to help them behave appropriately. These students, 1–5% of the student body, usually require intense, highly individualized support, provided by a team rather than a single expert, that focuses on the specific characteristics of their behavior and analysis of evidence from previous interventions and functional assessments. The goal at Tier 3 is not only to decrease the behaviors causing concern, but also to help the student build new replacement skills and behaviors. An administrator may need to meet these students at the beginning of each day to coach them and at the end of the day to review their successes and challenges.

Sometimes staff remove students from the areas in which they are having difficulty. For example, if a student has difficulty sitting near students, he or she may require an isolated desk. Similarly, a student who misbehaves with peers during recess may need to be isolated to a given area of the playground or be removed from recess altogether for a period of time. It will undoubtedly be necessary to teach these students the type of desired behaviors they need to succeed academically and socially at school.

You may be able to leverage community agencies to assist students and families. Referrals to school resource officers (specially trained sheriffs and police officers who work with schools in a community), social services, child protective services, or community-based counseling services may be helpful and necessary as each specific situation dictates. These outside resources can often bring more structures or supports to a child or family in need.

The most intensive of interventions may require information gleaned from a *functional analysis assessment* (FAA) or a *functional behavioral assessment* (FBA). These assessments use a variety of techniques to first diagnose the cause(s) of the behavior and then to identify interventions that might address the cause(s). They help us look beyond the symptom (the behavior) and to understand the student's underlying motivation to escape, avoid, or get something. For example, if a school team determines through a FAA or FBA that a student is seeking attention by acting out, the team can develop a plan to teach the student more appropriate ways to gain attention, thereby filling the student's need for attention with an alternative behavior that serves the same "function" as the inappropriate behavior. While FAAs and FBAs are usually completed for students with an IEP or as part of a formal evaluation, they can also be used for general education students at Tier 3. Specialists may be available to work with students and staff to help reinforce appropriate behavior structures.

Tier 3 behavioral interventions often include, but are not restricted to the following:

- *Adult mentorship*—Staff members serve as mentors in order to build or strengthen the connection between students and the school.

- *Social skills training*—Social skills have been found to be better predictors of eighth-grade academic achievement than third-grade test results (Caprara et. al, 2000).

- *Behavioral supports*—Positive reinforcements and evidence-based strategies are used in a small group setting with a low student-to-teacher ratio.

- *Self-monitoring*—Students become more aware of their own behavior by monitoring it at certain times of the day or in certain settings. Self-monitoring helps students to develop a stronger sense of self-determination.

If Tier 3 supports and interventions are ineffective, a referral to special education may be necessary. For students who already have an IEP, a recommendation for additional assessment and/or related services may be appropriate. There are specific, successful services for students in special education, particularly for those students with specifically diagnosed disabilities.

An effective PRTI will assist students with academic and behavioral concerns using the same structures and systems. IDEIA establishes legal, procedural, and compliance guidelines that must be addressed and followed. Schools' success in addressing these issues will help ensure they improve all students' learning and that they avoid due process and fair hearing problems. The next chapter focuses on steps schools can take.

Behavioral Interventions in Secondary School

Glenn W. Levey Middle School had a long history of academic failure. Located in the impoverished neighborhoods of Southfield, a suburb of Detroit, Michigan, the school ranked in the bottom 5% of all the state's public schools, with less than a third of its students proficient in reading, writing, and mathematics. Equally troubling, student behavior on campus was at a crisis level, averaging more than 3,000 disciplinary referrals and suspensions a year. When Dr. Anthony Muhammad was named principal, he knew his students were capable of high levels of learning. Although Dr. Muhammad was well-versed in PLC best practices, when he met with his leadership team to begin planning to improve student learning, he did not start focusing on collaborative time for teachers, essential standards, common assessments, or a systematic academic intervention program. Instead, he knew that until the school created a safe, orderly campus that addressed students' social and emotional needs, it could not address their academic needs. What Levey's students needed first was a system of behavioral interventions.

Tier 1

To address this issue, the Levey staff utilized PLC practices, starting with creating shared knowledge through collective inquiry. Dr. Muhammad and the leadership team created a "teacher curriculum," in which the entire staff learned about the traits of highly effective middle schools and the developmental needs of adolescent students. The staff also dug deeply into Levey's disciplinary data, looking for trends in student conduct and leverage points to focus their initial improvement efforts. From this study, the school created a list of student conduct expectations, delineated by student actions that were "non-negotiable" and developmentally appropriate for adolescents. These behavioral expectations were taught to the students and reinforced in a schoolwide character education program that was implemented during student advisory time. Additionally, because the staff noticed that many of the previous year's student-to-student conflicts happened during transition times between classes, the school revised their class schedule to limit student contact time during passing periods. To improve the communication and relations between the school and parents, Levey hired a parent volunteer coordinator. Combined, these actions helped shore up the school's behavioral core program.

Tier 2

To identify students in need of supplemental support, the Levey staff created a clear, consistent, and fair process to hold all students accountable to the school's behavioral expectations. These steps included all staff members and addressed both rewards and privileges for positive behavior choices and targeted consequences for inappropriate actions. Because some students needed additional time and support to meet the school's expectations, the counseling staff developed an intervention plan to assist students who had social needs that could interfere with their academic success. In addition, the administration hired "student support specialists" to ensure that no student would fail. Because many students lacked positive connections to the community, service learning projects were implemented throughout the building. Partnerships were established with the University of Michigan, Michigan State University, and Oakland University in order to expose Levey students to college-prep opportunities.

Tier 3

While these Tier 2 interventions were highly effective, a small handful of students needed extremely intensive Tier 3 interventions. Students at this level attended a parent-administrator meeting at which a conduct contract was written that clearly outlined the targeted behaviors, the support for changing behavior, and the consequences if the student's behavior did not improve. If the contract was violated, the student was referred to an alternative program in the district.

These steps by the Levey staff have proven to be very successful. Within 3 years, the school's suspensions were down from over 3,000 during the 2001–2002 school year to 148 in 2004–2005. In the 2004–2005 school year, 52% of Levey students were on the honor roll, and 18 charitable student service learning projects were completed. Because Levey's behavior interventions worked hand-in-hand with the school's academic interventions, the school has seen a tremendous growth in student learning. Levey was named a National School of Excellence by the U.S. Department of Education in 2004, and its state test scores rank in the top 5% in Michigan.

What are your behavioral interventions?

See page 191 for an activity to help your leadership team evaluate your behavioral interventions. Discuss each element that should be found in a behavioral intervention program, and honestly record your current reality. Next, record your long-term desired outcome, and establish a few short-term goals.

See page 192 for "Functional Behavior Analysis Protocol." This activity will help you to identify, understand, and analyze a specific problem behavior and find a replacement behavior.

Visit **go.solution-tree.com/rti**
to download these activities.

Chapter Ten

Meeting Legal Requirements

*The single biggest problem in communication
is the illusion that it has taken place.*

—George Bernard Shaw

Jeremy, a third grader at Magnolia Elementary School, has struggled for the past 2 years. A student study team (SST) met with his mom last year, when Jeremy was in second grade, but no follow-up meeting has yet occurred.

For the first 4 months of third grade, Jeremy made little progress. He was encouraged to attend after-school tutoring sessions, but baseball practice often prevented him from doing so. His teacher, Mrs. Campbell, requested that Jeremy sit at the front of the room and reduced his homework load, but to no avail. The school's administrative team discussed whether special education, or at least formal evaluation, might be a good idea for him. But then, as Magnolia developed a PRTI, the student study team (SST) became "gung ho" about behaving like a professional learning community.

So for the next 5 months, an instructor pulled Jeremy out of Mrs. Campbell's class in the afternoons to receive assistance with fluency and comprehension; the team began with those two areas based on Jeremy's low percentile on the standardized reading test. The program used appeared to work well, although the research base on it was inadequate.

Today, Jeremy seems to be performing better in class; he is also turning in more homework, completing a little more classwork, and performing better on his weekly spelling tests. Mrs. Campbell senses that his score may improve on the state tests given in the spring. However, the SST lately has been concerned that Jeremy does not sound as though he is reading aloud better; during small-group guided reading, he still seems confused when asked about the story that his reading group is discussing.

Mrs. Campbell decided to schedule a meeting to discuss the support the staff has provided and the progress Jeremy has made over the past 9 months, as well as the possibility of special education testing. His mother attended the meeting and listened carefully. After not arriving at a decision, the SST arranged to meet again in a week. Jeremy's mother returned then, accompanied by an advocate. They had many questions, particularly concerning the many discrepancies between the support Jeremy has been receiving and IDEIA's and the state's special education regulations.

"Why didn't you contact me sooner?" Jeremy's mother asked. "I feel like no one from this school ever communicates with me."

"Why wasn't the option of formal evaluation to determine special education eligibility discussed with Jeremy's mother?" the advocate demanded.

"Well, I thought that's why we were meeting today," Mrs. Campbell stuttered.

"The reading program seemed to be working," the principal said defensively.

"Is that program research-based?" the advocate asked. "Did you use assessments to determine if Jeremy's progress was adequate?"

Magnolia's team members looked at each other nervously, wishing they had met with Jeremy's mother a little sooner.

Keys to Compliance

A thoughtfully designed pyramid response to intervention helps ensure that schools meet all student learning needs and that students who are experiencing difficulty receive systematic interventions. A school that operates as a professional learning community can be particularly effective at helping students achieve academic excellence if its PRTI includes:

- Early preventative services

- Multiple tiers to meet increasingly intensive deficiencies

- Diagnostic, explicit programs to meet specific needs

However, IDEIA 2004 introduces additional considerations. This federal special education law justifiably compels schools and schools' support systems to meet the criteria that will be discussed in this chapter. A high-quality PRTI can meet student needs before a formal evaluation, but the documentation and communication required by IDEIA, which allows and encourages RTI and systematic early intervening services (EIS) for K–3 students, must be taken seriously and completed carefully.

The Council for Exceptional Children's Division for Learning Disabilities, the International Reading Association, the Learning Disabilities Association of America, the National Center for Learning Disabilities, and the National Education Association have all cautioned their members against violating student rights under IDEIA regulations. Among their shared concerns are: not involving parents early and often enough and not advising parents of their rights under IDEIA; using intervention programs that are not research-based; and using progress-monitoring assessments that are not valid and reliable.

Among other considerations, school systems and schools should determine their response to the following requirements in order to comply with IDEIA and other federal regulations:

1. Develop a systematic progress-monitoring plan.

2. Keep careful records.

3. Utilize research-based programs.

4. Change a student's tier when appropriate.

5. Refer for formal evaluation when appropriate.

6. Meet periodically with all stakeholders, including parents.

SSTs that attend to these considerations will make intelligent decisions that are in a child's best interest—and will steer clear of compliance violations that may lead parents to make a legal complaint against the school district, a possibility facing the team at Jeremy's school. When these issues are not addressed, parents and guardians might file motions for due process or fair hearing. Their questions often include:

- "What does my child need at this point?"

- "What type of work are you doing with him?"

- "How will we know if he is showing improvement and improving at a rate that will close the gap between present performance and grade-level standards?"

- "What will the school do if he is not improving?"

- "How long will the school wait before trying a different type of assistance?"

- "If my child were in special education, what other types of assistance could he receive?"

- "Are all the staff who work with him highly qualified, adequately credentialed, and otherwise trained?

- "Are the programs being used with my child research-based and proven to be effective?"

- "How often will the school communicate with my family?"

Parents and guardians of students with IEPs may heartily welcome IDEIA regulations, particularly those who fail to receive updates on their children's progress more than annually or who may not know the types and quality of programs teachers use with their children. They also usually appreciate a PRTI system's use of research-based programs and its frequent progress monitoring. And parents of children who exhibit characteristics of high-incidence disabilities (for example, specific learning disabilities or speech and language impairment) will probably greatly appreciate the early intervention that PRTI offers. Parents are anxious that schools really will consider carefully their children's best interests and assign them to appropriate interventions as soon as possible.

Develop a Systematic Progress-Monitoring Plan

It is not enough to design a PRTI, ensure the students who most need assistance attend interventions, assign the very best instructors, and utilize diagnostic, explicit, and systematic programs. In addition, educators must ask: Are students responding to interventions by progressing *enough* in their learning? That is, does the student's performance place him or her above the 24th percentile; is the student's improved performance above pre-established criteria; is the student's slope of improvement comparable to peers; or is the student's progress on track to achieve grade-level proficiency?

Successful intervention programs periodically gauge student progress. Valuable internal instruments that assess student progress should be accompanied by external ones, such as DIBELS or the Qualitative Reading Inventory (QRI). Using external assessments will allow schools to monitor student progress and the efficacy of the interventions. Literacy educators can use these tools to assess students' progress in phonemic awareness, phonics, fluency, and comprehension; these tools also help educators listen to and record students' reading ability. Teams must use such instruments every 1–2 weeks for students in Tier 3 and every 3–4 weeks for students in Tier 2. In addition, educators can diagnose students' ongoing needs based on data from these assessments, a process that may lead to more targeted and successful interventions. Finally, assessment data can reveal the interventions' effectiveness and the fidelity with which educators implement them.

In developing a systemic, progress-monitoring plan, an SST should schedule frequent, short, formative assessments that inform its decisions about future work with each student, particularly in terms of choosing programs that respond to the child's areas of deficiency. The team should regularly share the results of these probes with all stakeholders.

Keep Careful Records

Educators should record the results of their regular progress monitoring in a clear, organized way, so that administrators, psychologists, teachers, and parents can readily understand the data. First, staff should record the dates when specific programs are initiated, what their frequency and duration are, and what student needs they are trying to meet. An individualized learning plan record sheet includes a student's past assessment data and provides space to record the scores of the current year's progress monitoring. Curriculum-based measurement (CBM) and DIBELS provide record sheets within the progress-monitoring booklets themselves. They also list the academic goal (for example, a certain number of words read correctly in a minute) that students are expected to reach by year's end. Using these kinds of brief assessments, educators can regularly plot a student's scores and understand his or her progress—or lack thereof.

Second, educators should record the dates of team meetings at which students are discussed and the dates of the school's communication with parents when they make changes in a student's intervention plan. Write down or record electronically the notes teachers made during instruction and the assessment tools they utilized. For example, an effective student record sheet for a student who does not seem able to retain and utilize sounds and sound blends will record, evaluate, and share instances when the student drops word endings, demonstrates weak knowledge of sight words, or demonstrates a weaker inferential comprehension than explicit comprehension. Using this knowledge, the staff can adjust instruction to maximize the student's learning.

School teams would be wise to use IEPs from special education, which are legally compliant documents, as a model for these records.

Utilize Research-Based Programs

The National Reading Panel (National Institute of Child Health and Human Development, 2000) and the President's Commission on Excellence in Special Education (2002), among other organizations, have stressed the importance of high-quality, research-based programs and interventions. Schools and districts have been found legally at fault when they have utilized programs that lacked this research base with children with IEPs.

Pyramid response to intervention must follow these same guidelines to serve students well and to avoid procedural errors and the legal challenges that may ensue. The What Works Clearinghouse, initiated in 2002 and supported by the U.S. Department of Education, provides educators with information about programs that have been proven to work well with children in specific content areas (U.S. Department of Education's Institute of Education Sciences, 2008). At press time, this site had reviewed 24 programs in beginning reading, including the areas of alphabetics, fluency, comprehension, and general reading achievement.

The Florida Center for Reading Research, established in 2002, conducts scientific research on reading and disseminates information about research-based practices. As of early 2008, it provided extensive informa-

tion on 94 reading programs. The Oregon Reading First Center (www.
oregonreadingfirst.uoregon.edu) also provides extensive research on and
reviews of reading programs. Schools will benefit from using this research
to select programs for a PRTI and to explain these programs' content and
research base to teachers, parents, and other interested parties.

Staff should evaluate intervention programs in terms of whether they
are systematic and explicit, according to the following criteria:

- All stakeholders can readily understand the
  learning objectives of program lessons.

- Programs include lesson dialogues between students and
  teachers and provide clear instructional directions.

- Pacing is balanced (neither too fast or slow), and frequent
  dialogue occurs between teacher and students.

- Instructors use scaffolding, in which previously mastered
  concepts form the foundation for new ones.

- Instructors introduce new skills sequentially and break down
  bigger ideas into smaller, more manageable information.

- Lessons develop with a well-articulated scope and
  sequence, new topics are introduced thoroughly,
  and prior concepts are periodically reviewed.

- Instructors have ample opportunities to provide
  clear, concise instruction and model the successful
  application of new learning skills.

- Students have enough time to practice what they have learned.

- Cumulative reviews occur periodically so that
  students revisit and relearn new skills.

- Essential skills are linked and integrated.

All interventions considered for a PRTI should meet these criteria.

Another important consideration is the amount of time required to
complete the intervention program on a daily basis. This will be essential
in planning intervention schedules. Compared to intervention programs
that address all the same components as the Tier 1 core, more focused
interventions typically target a limited number of skills (for example,
fluency) and can be completed in a more limited time frame (25–30

minutes). Some intervention programs that claim to be supplemental may in fact supplant the Tier 1 core program; such supplanting is only appropriate for students who are significantly below grade-level proficiency. Programs that supplant the core program are more common in grades 4 and up than in grades K–3.

Change Tiers When Appropriate

A balance must be struck between allowing sufficient time for intervention programs to work and moving students to more targeted and intensive tiers when it is evident they are not responding to less rigorous supports. The urge to continue intervening in Tier 2 may be particularly strong among a group of professionals who have worked hard to develop and implement a PRTI and who are emotionally invested in the success of students and their system. Nonetheless, guidelines exist that suggest when movement to more intensive tiers is appropriate. Most researchers recommend that decisions about whether to exit students from the current level should be made after 6–8 weeks of intervention (Batsche et al., 2006; Brown-Chidsey & Steege, 2005; Fuchs & Fuchs, 2005; Fuchs & Fuchs, 2006, 2007). Violating these agreed-upon norms for when more intensive supports should be provided may result in due process complaints for delaying special education services.

If a student has responded well to interventions, he or she can be returned to a less intensive level of intervention. However, if the student has made adequate progress but the team determines that more time in the current tier is required, then the student's services may remain the same. And when the student makes little or no progress, he or she might need to move to a more intensive tier.

Fuchs and Fuchs (2007) describe four options to determine whether a response is adequate:

1. The student is above the 24th percentile at the end of the 6–8 week time period.

2. The team considers her performance at grade level, as defined by a criterion-based assessment, for example, when the student's QRI or the DIBELS Oral Reading Fluency reveals that she is meeting grade-level standards.

3. The student's slope of improvement indicates that she is on track to achieve grade-level proficiency.

4. Instructors combine a student's slope of progress and end-of-intervention performance to indicate that the child has not responded to intervention and thus needs to move to a more intensive tier.

Again, all team members, including parents, should understand data about the student and clearly communicate their interpretation of it.

Refer for Formal Evaluation

Parent advocacy groups have published brief reports that encourage parents to be aware of RTI. For example, the Council for Exceptional Children's published position on RTI includes three key cautions: 1) RTI initiatives should be schoolwide; 2) they should involve a partnership between general education, special education, and parents; and 3) they should not delay the referral of a child who is suspected of having a learning disability for formal evaluation (Council for Exceptional Children, 2007). While this report and others are supportive of RTI, they caution parents to know their rights and to ensure that schools correctly design and implement intervention systems. To satisfy parents' and guardians' needs, staff also must see to it that interventions do not unnecessarily delay special education services.

Experts agree that the formal evaluation of students and the special education services that may result have not been highly successful (Shaywitz, 2003; Fuchs & Fuchs, 2007). However, schools risk litigation if parents perceive that educators are reluctant to assess their children and instead retain them in an intervention. If students have not responded to the interventions prescribed by a well-designed and well-implemented PRTI system, then the team must explain other options, including referring them to a higher tier or to special education assessment.

Many states' special education regulations allow an evaluation team 60 days to determine a child's eligibility for special education, as well as the student's areas of deficit and the services he or she requires. Using the data and information gathered, recorded, and analyzed during a PRTI, decisions can be much better informed and timely than within a 60-day evaluation period. Assuming that a SST has met regularly, its decision to formally assess a child should be the logical next step in the team's tiered response to the child's needs. Yet problems may arise when educators' communication with each other and the student's family has been irregular, unclear, or inconsistent. The process also may not run smoothly if parents request formal assessment before the team agrees or before educators implement a well-designed PRTI system.

Many states' special education regulations require schools to formally assess students whenever a parent requests such an evaluation in writing. (It is unclear whether governmental regulations adopted since IDEIA 2004 will change this provision.) Schools that implement PRTI can respond to early parental requests with a systematic plan for helping a child to learn. Parent advocacy groups will feel reassured when educators routinely refer students for formal evaluation after they have experienced all of the Tier 3 intensive services available to them.

Meet Periodically With All Stakeholders

Communication between schools and parents or guardians is key; in fact, *communication is the most critical issue identified in this chapter.* Every 6–8 weeks, after they have provided a significant amount of intervention to a student, teams should meet with parents to discuss the student's progress. Parents and guardians will embrace PRTI if educators tell them what has been done for their child to date and what will be attempted in the future and provide parents an opportunity to ask questions and make suggestions. Serious disagreements can be avoided when parents truly believe that the school is doing whatever it takes for their children.

Five Steps to Good Communication

The following steps will ensure that you treat all stakeholders respectfully and show them that you consider them intelligent enough to understand the difficulties that children experience and how the school's methods help improve students' learning.

1. Explain how the school has systematically monitored the child's progress. Show parents their child's assessments, and explain how they are administered and what they reveal about the student.

2. Share the records of past student performance that the school has maintained; explain the data honestly, and use it to relate the story of the student's progress.

3. Describe why the team elected certain interventions and how it judged a program to be an appropriate prescription for a student's diagnosed needs. Show all team members the programs, and briefly explain how they work.

4. Reveal how data supports the team's recommendations to give a student more time in a given tier or to change tiers.

5. Make specific recommendations, but be open to input from parents and guardians.

Lastly, keep in mind that parents and students have rights and that a referral for formal evaluation may be necessary if the student is not responding to interventions or if other symptoms of a learning disability are present. Formal evaluation to determine eligibility for special education should not be avoided or delayed.

Making the Commitment to Go From Good to Great

In 25 years, we may reflect that the decision to create individual educational goals and learning plans for every student was the most significant movement in public education during the past several decades. By adopting pyramid response to intervention, a school becomes better managed and maximizes student learning; a staff committed to professional learning communities shares a common commitment to *all* children. In fact, the process of differentiating curriculum, time, and support to promote every student's academic growth is nothing less than groundbreaking.

A school can greatly enhance a child's achievement when it places a high-quality teacher in his or her classroom, and when it maximizes instructional time and otherwise intelligently uses intervention programs. Yet the question remains: What will the school do when a student remains at risk? Educators need to respond diagnostically, systematically, and with a sense of urgency when the adopted curricula and state standards prove too difficult for the child. Schools will move from good to great when they firmly commit to doing everything required, including modifying existing interventions, to help students learn. PLCs and RTI provide the framework to support this commitment.

Following the advice in this book will not, in and of itself, ensure IDEIA compliance. State regulations are quite varied, and some states have not produced regulations at all. Still, schools and school leaders should consider these questions:

- When does your staff share procedural safeguards? Answer this question even if you believe you regularly involve parents in their children's education and generally respect and protect parents' and their children's rights under IDEIA.

- Do you offer parents the right to request formal evaluation to determine if a student is eligible for special education before initiating any interventions or support within the PRTI? Although you must respect parents' right to request such evaluation, particularly if staff suspects a student disability, you should also consider whether a formal assessment might be premature.

Recall the Heartland Area Education Agency (HAEA) example in chapter 3. Since the late 1980s, HAEA has been practicing a model RTI system with more students, and for a longer period of time, than almost any other district in the United States. HAEA schools also meaningfully involve parents, beginning with the problem-solving team meetings at which a child is initially identified as a candidate for comprehensive interventions.

A thorough evaluation, as delineated in state regulations, requires that team decisions for placement in special education are based on a body of evidence that reveals three possibilities:

1. A student has not responded to interventions at an acceptable rate, or the level of intensity of services is too demanding to continue without special education services.

2. Even with additional supports, a significant discrepancy exists between a student's performance and that of peers or of grade-level standards.

3. The team believes that the child has instructional needs that cannot be met in a supplemented general education environment and has identified different environmental conditions and supports that will meet those needs.

If a team determines the student qualifies for special education services, its decision as to what programs to utilize presents both a challenge and an opportunity. The challenge is that although special education teacher teams may use high-quality interventions, students may not respond well to them—sometimes because they are the same programs, or the same types of programs, to which students did not respond previously. The opportunity is that resource programs can serve students in a more targeted and individualized manner, which may have been the intent of special education in the first place. This kind of approach contrasts with many of today's resource programs, which tend to have a one-size-fits-all approach, rather than one based on a child's specifically diagnosed needs.

Within a PRTI, schools come to know what has and has not worked with a particular student and so better understand his or her needs. Staff must use this personal knowledge, and that acquired during the formal evaluation process, to design more diagnostically tailored plans, which staff must monitor periodically to determine their efficacy, even when students are receiving special education services.

In deciding who is responsible for directing the systematic interventions that they design and employ, educators must think beyond the traditional division between regular and special education. Rather, *all* educators and administrators must take responsibility for a PRTI. Principals in particular must fully assume their roles as instructional leaders and commit themselves to leading and managing well-planned and well-executed interventions.

It would be a shame if intervening early with students were to cost schools legally and financially. Yet if schools commit the procedural errors identified in Jeremy's story at the beginning of this chapter, parents and advocates might respond with due-process and fair-hearing demands.

A pyramid response to intervention will only be as successful as the school's planning and procedures. Again, a PRTI system will not reach its true potential without:

- Research-based programs
- A systematic progress-monitoring plan
- Careful record-keeping
- Processes for teams to change students' tiers of intervention when appropriate, and to refer children to formal evaluation
- Regular meetings involving all stakeholders

Failure to include and adhere to these elements can violate IDEIA requirements and increase fair-hearing filings.

Now that we understand Tiers 1, 2, and 3, as well as behavioral and legal considerations, we are ready to put it all together.

How will you coordinate, document, and communicate about your PRTI?

See page 194 for an activity to help your leadership team ensure that you maintain a compliant PRTI. Discuss key questions for coordination, documentation, and communication while providing a solid program at Tiers 1, 2, and 3. Then record your current and desired practices in relation to each item.

Visit **go.solution-tree.com/rti**
to download this activity.

Chapter Eleven
Putting It All Together

*Do not wait; the time will never be "just right." Start where
you stand, and work with whatever tools you may have at your
command, and better tools will be found as you go along.*

—Napoleon Hill, American speaker and motivational writer

To help their students at risk avoid failing, Sycamore High School educators created a PRTI system. At the end of the first quarter, Joe Smith, a teacher, referred one of his students, Tim O'Brian, for intervention support because Tim was failing his biology class.

After meeting with Tim, Nancy Chu, the school counselor and Tim's intervention coordinator, assigned him to daily after-school study hall. "There are still 9 weeks left in the semester to improve your grade," Ms. Chu reminded Tim.

Tim leaned back in his chair and announced, "Yeah, well, I don't plan on doing anything else until next semester."

"But you have to pass science to earn enough credits to graduate!" Ms. Chu exclaimed.

"You just don't get it, do you?" Tim said. "There's no way I can pass biology. I have a 22% right now, and Mr. Smith doesn't accept make-up work, extra credit, or make-up tests. Even if I earn every point possible for the second quarter, I still can't pass, so why try?"

Avoiding Pitfalls

Unfortunately, Tim was right. As the 10th-grade PRTI coordinator, Ms. Chu was at a loss; although she had numerous interventions at her disposal, none of them could help Tim, given Mr. Smith's grading practices. As Jeff's situation demonstrates, a PRTI cannot be a stand-alone program; instead, it must be part of a schoolwide focus on learning and, as such, will only be truly effective if *all* school practices are aligned to support student achievement.

The following factors can undermine PRTI systems:

- Counterproductive grading practices

- Failure to communicate program goals and procedures to students and parents

- Lack of program evaluation

Counterproductive Grading Practices

Tim's story demonstrates that grading practices can greatly affect the extent of student learning. Unfortunately, traditional approaches to grading are all too often counterproductive to the objective of maximizing learning for all students (O'Connor, 2007). This conflict exists because most current grading procedures are designed to sort and rank student achievement; they reward students who learn quickly and accurately and punish those who require additional time and opportunities to master material.

PRTI systems often use student grades to identify students in need of additional support. Yet because most teachers have complete autonomy over their grading practices, significant differences exist among them on what a grade actually represents. For example, imagine that two U.S. history teachers, Mr. Fiora and Ms. Cohen, work on the same school departmental team. While they have agreed to teach the same essential learning standards and to give common assessments, they have vastly different procedures for determining grades. Mr. Fiora makes test scores

40% of a student's final grade, grades tests on a curve, and gives extra credit to students who attend local civic events. In Ms. Cohen's class, exam results constitute 80% of a student's final grade, tests are scored on a traditional percentage scale, and no extra credit is available.

At the end of the first semester, two students (one from Mr. Fiora's class and one from Ms. Cohen's) each received a score of 60% on the departmental final exam. Because the exam measured the essential material that students learned, one might assume that the two students demonstrated similar mastery of the material. But Mr. Fiora's student received a semester grade of A-, while Ms. Cohen's received a D.

Why this huge discrepancy? On the whole, Mr. Fiora's students did poorly on the final, so his curved grade for 60% correct on this exam was a C. But his student earned all the points possible for homework and received extra credit for attending a local school board meeting, which brought up his final grade for Mr. Fiora's class to an A-. On the other hand, the 60% correct on the final in Ms. Cohen's class earned her student a D- for the test. With such a heavy weight on test scores and no opportunities for extra credit, Ms. Cohen's student received a D as a final grade.

The point of this illustration is not to judge which grading system is better, but to illustrate the effects that grading discrepancies can have on a school PRTI. Ms. Cohen likely will recommend her student for extra support because the student's semester grade puts her in danger of failing. On the other hand, Mr. Fiora's student not only is unlikely to be recommended for extra help, but with a final grade of A-, he could be eligible for the honor roll. Thus, quite a gap exists between two students who demonstrate the same level of learning mastery on the semester summative common assessment.

Besides measuring student learning, grading practices also have a tremendous impact on student attitudes and motivation. According to educational assessment expert Anne Davies (2007), a student's motivation is so important to student achievement that it is a cornerstone in designing an effective school assessment program. Grading practices have the power to inspire or extinguish a student's desire to learn, especially in situations in which he or she already has done poorly. For example, consider a student who fails an essential learning assessment in mathematics and whom the school refers to its PRTI program to receive additional instruction. At the end of this intervention, after the student successfully demonstrates mastery of the material, his teacher informs the child that his initial grade will still be his final grade. This grading policy hardly reflects the student's ultimate proficiency level. Equally important, the student probably will not attend future interventions, given that his prior effort has no impact upon his final grade. As Thomas Guskey (2007) notes:

> If teachers follow assessments with high-quality corrective instruction, then students should have a second chance to demonstrate their new level of competence and understanding. This second chance determines the effectiveness of the corrective process while also giving students another opportunity to experience success in learning, thus providing them with additional motivation. (p. 23)

If one of a PRTI's purposes is to ensure all students the additional time and support they need to master essential learning, then a school's grading practices shouldn't undermine these ends.

Ultimately, the question comes down to: What is the purpose of grading? If it is to sort students by their speed of learning, their level of prior knowledge, or their ability to benefit from a teacher's teaching strategies, then traditional grading practices work perfectly. However, if the purpose of grades is to accurately represent student learning, then we must revise our practices to better serve this purpose. As Ken O'Connor (2007) states, "We must adopt grading practices that are more compatible with an emphasis on learning. To do this, we must have a shared vision of the primary purpose of grades: To provide communication in summary format about student achievement in meeting learning goals" (p. 128).

Failure to Communicate Program Goals and Procedures to Students and Parents

Schools that design and implement a PRTI often fail to communicate the system's goals and procedures to students and parents. While we might assume that offering extra help to students would be embraced by them and their parents, they may not, if the school does not also clearly articulate how the program works and what its aims are. Potential pitfalls in communication include students' and parents' perceptions of the intervention as either punitive or remedial.

Punitive perceptions stem from cases in which students, having been referred for interventions, feel that they are "in trouble." Children may well already find it stressful and anxiety-producing to meet with an administrator or counselor regarding insufficient academic achievement. These feelings detract from the goal of developing positive, supportive relationships with students that can help them build confidence and achieve greater success. For this reason, staff should teach students and parents about PRTI's decidedly nonpunitive purpose *before* referring a student to an intervention program. And when the student is referred, staff members should assure him or her with such statements as:

- "You're not in trouble."
- "We're concerned about your current progress, and we are here to help."
- "Everyone needs extra help sometimes."
- "We care about you so much, we won't let you fail."
- "We're going to do whatever it takes until you're more successful."

Of course, the school should share the same information about the PRTI with the child's parents or guardians by sending them a personalized letter and/or inviting them to a PRTI informational meeting. Staffs that fail to do so risk losing parents' support for their child's assigned interventions.

For example, suppose a school PRTI coordinator assigned a student to attend an after-school science tutorial. Later that day, the coordinator receives an angry call from the child's parent, who requests justification for why the child was placed "in detention." Although the parent was misinformed, she did not make an unreasonable leap in logic to assume that the child's detention after school was a disciplinary consequence. Through proactive communication, the school could have avoided this problem.

Another common misperception by students and parents is that a school's PRTI system is a remedial program designed solely for students who are significantly below grade level. Parents may assume that their child's placement in a PRTI intervention puts him on a substandard track of study, thus potentially labeling the student and limiting his future access to higher levels of coursework.

In traditional schools, this assumption is based upon past reality, for their academic support programs generally create these detrimental outcomes. To address this concern, the school should promptly inform parents that children's placement in the PRTI system is designed to help them succeed in grade-level curricula.

In the end, school leaders must understand that most parents and students are unaccustomed to a school that takes full responsibility for student learning and provides a systemic support process to ensure that all students succeed. When a school does not consciously and consistently communicate its plans, parents and students can misinterpret an intervention as punitive or unjust. Once such misperceptions are created, they are extremely difficult to change.

Lack of Program Evaluation

Chapter 4 notes that one of a PLC's guiding principles is to focus on results—that is, a professional learning community does not hope its students will learn, but instead seeks specific evidence that its instructional practices and procedures support high levels of learning for all students. Unfortunately, program evaluation is a frequently forgotten aspect of RTI planning.

As part of the PRTI process, educators should ask themselves whether the following statements are true of their school:

- We are accurately identifying students who need additional support.

- Our identification process is timely enough to help students before they get too far behind.

- We know whether a student is receiving interventions suitable for him or her.

- We know that each individual intervention program is research-based and highly effective.

- Our teachers are implementing our interventions with fidelity and efficacy.

- We know when a student is ready to exit the program.

In addition, staff has to determine how to assess student and parent perceptions of the program. Remember that building an effective PRTI system is not a single act, but an ongoing, fluid process. By digging deeply into these critical questions, a school can design assessments that contribute to future program effectiveness. In fact, a PRTI system should not only help students, but also educators, to continually learn and improve.

Leadership Matters

The principal's role in implementing a pyramid response to intervention is critical to its success. The day is long gone when the fate of the school's neediest learners simply was relegated to the school psychologist and to student study teams.

If a school's PRTI is to be effective, especially with students needing intensive help, the principal must be the leader of the process, the "head learner" (Barth, 1990, p. 162). If the principal completely delegates to others his or her responsibility to oversee the pyramid of interventions—especially at the Tier 3 intensive level where needs are most severe—then teachers receive the message that the administration places a low priority on the process and does not view it as central to ensuring that all students learn. As DuFour, DuFour, Eaker, and Many (2006) note in *Learning by Doing*:

> John Gardner (1988) once observed that "the impulse of most leaders is much the same today as it was a thousand years ago: accept the system as it is and lead it" (p. 24). Those who hope to serve in any leadership capacity in building PLCs must overcome that impulse. They must help people break free of the thicket of precedent, the tangle of unquestioned assumptions, and the trap of comfortable complacency. Their task is not only to help people throughout the organization acquire the knowledge and skills to solve the intractable challenges of today, but also to develop their capacity and confidence to tackle the unforeseen challenges that will emerge in the future. No program, no textbook, no curriculum, no technology will be sufficient to meet this challenge. Educators will remain the most important resource in the battle to provide every child with a quality education, and thus leaders must commit to creating the conditions in which those educators can continue to grow and learn as professionals. (p. 185)

Schools need leaders more than ever. If we view our schools and our nation as in the midst of "the perfect storm," then it logically follows that no ship could ever sail through such challenging seas without the steady hand and committed leadership of the ship's captain. Schools can and will be successful when the principal *leads* them through and beyond today's challenges rather than being "tossed about" on stormy waters as just another passenger. The school principal must assume the role of advocate for all students, so that all students achieve at high levels.

Success Stories

The following three stories illustrate how an elementary school, a middle school, and a high school district "put it all together" to create successful PRTI systems. These models are offered not as prescriptions to apply exactly as described, but rather as examples to stimulate your thinking about how such successes might be accomplished in states with varying interpretations of RTI regulations and in schools with widely varying cultures and structures.

R. H. Dana Elementary School

R. H. Dana Elementary School, located south of Los Angeles, developed a PRTI to ensure that every student reaches high levels of proficiency in literacy and mathematics through a diagnose-and-prescribe strategy. The school constantly diagnoses student needs and prescribes increasingly targeted supports. R. H. Dana's first and ongoing goal is to strengthen the core curriculum. Reading, writing, and mathematics are the primary focus of teaching and learning, taking up between 80–85% of the instructional minutes each day.

Tier 1

The staff has identified power standards in mathematics. They have also made a commitment to significant writing every day and focus on key genres and applications. They ensure that all aspects of the literacy curriculum, from phonemic awareness to comprehension, are covered in the scope and sequence of K–5 reading instruction, in part by using the adopted balanced literacy curriculum with fidelity. Staff members visit other classrooms regularly during action walks to ensure consistency in practice and expectations across all classrooms. The principal visits every classroom every day to provide support and to supervise that curricula are used appropriately and that instructional time is maximized. Results have been positive, and all the more impressive given that more than 75% of students qualify for free or reduced price lunch, over 70% of students are from an ethnic minority (Latino), and more than 60% of students are classified as English learners.

Universal Screening

All students are universally screened at least three times a year with DIBELS and the Qualitative Reading Inventory (QRI). Students reading below grade are further diagnosed to identify their exact needs so that supplemental supports they will receive in Tiers 2 and 3 are targeted and successful. Grade-level teacher teams give students common writing assignments that they collaboratively grade and develop their own math assessments based on power standards that they analyze for gaps in learning. They use commercially produced unit assessments that externally validate student learning in reading. These assessments help identify gaps in classwide learning and further identify individuals who need additional time and support.

Tier 1 Differentiated Support

An absolutely essential component of the Tier 1 program is differentiated support in the classroom. Classroom teachers must schedule time to meet with small groups of students within normal class time. These small groups are flexibly formed—teachers pull together students with similar needs and then preteach skills for a future lesson, review content from past lessons for a second time, reteach key standards that were not mastered on earlier benchmark examinations, or provide enrichment to students who have exceeded content area expectations. Differentiation is part of the Tier 1 program at R. H. Dana, and it is the responsibility of the classroom teacher.

Professional development is focused on instructional strategies for reading, writing, and mathematics; maximizing instructional time; identifying power standards; and evaluating student work. But perhaps the most significant staff development involves strategies to organize and manage a classroom so that teachers can effectively meet with small groups of students.

Tier 2

Students in all grades who require supplemental support are taught with other students with similar needs in a reading room by highly trained interventionists. Based on the universal screening of students' literacy skills, immediate, targeted, explicit, and systematic intervention is provided based on diagnosed needs. The school has selected research-proven programs in each area of literacy. These interventions do not supplant the core curriculum; while students go to a reading room to receive pull-out interventions, they do not miss core instruction. For example, a fourth-grade student who requires a comprehension intervention would leave class when small groups rotate through differentiated time with their teacher and other students are working independently. When students in need of intervention would otherwise be engaged in independent work, they visit the reading room for additional support. By scheduling carefully, these students at risk can receive small-group support from their classroom teacher and targeted Tier 2 supports in the Reading Room.

A well-organized schedule is needed to accommodate the Tier 2 interventions and plan the instructional day around when students will be pulled out of class. Differentiated time in the classroom, when groups of students receive targeted instruction from their teacher in small, flexible groups, and other students work independently, is the best option for a classroom activity while pullouts are taking place. English language development support (ELDS) is provided during the day as a pull-out intervention and after school. Transportation is provided to those students who need it through an after-school grant from the state. Table 11-1 (page 149) shows the schoolwide instructional schedule.

Progress Monitoring

R. H. Dana students are assessed at least every 2 weeks with DIBELS to monitor progress in decoding and fluency, and with the QRI to monitor progress in decoding and comprehension. Data is recorded, displayed, and shared (with students, parents, interventionists, and teachers) on a graph that illustrates their progress toward grade-level goals. Students not responding adequately to interventions (defined as not reaching grade-level expectations or not progressing at a rate commensurate with peers who *are* successfully responding) receive different and additional support, and are considered for additional interventions and a higher tier. Students reaching grade-level expectations and maintaining this level are graduated from the intervention system, although they continue to be carefully monitored. The school's intervention team—comprised of the principal, reading specialist, resource specialist, and counselor—meets every other week to discuss students and data. The results of progress monitoring are shared in real time with classroom teachers. The school meets with parents

Table 11-1: The Instructional Schedule at R. H. Dana Elementary School

Time	Kindergarten	Time	First Grade	Time	Second and Third Grades	Time	Fourth and Fifth Grades
7:45	Whole-class decoding and comprehension and differentiated workshop	7:45	Whole-class decoding and comprehension and differentiated workshop	7:45	Spelling, vocabulary, and decoding	7:45	Spelling, vocabulary, and decoding
				8:10	Comprehension and differentiated workshop with comprehension and fluency pullouts	8:20	Comprehension and differentiated workshop with comprehension and fluency pullouts
9:43	Recess	9:43	Recess	9:43	Recess	10:03	Recess
10:00	Writing and conventions	10:00	Social studies, science, read aloud, and shared reading with decoding and comprehension pullouts	10:00	Writing and conventions with decoding pullout	10:20	Math
11:00	Lunch	11:20	Lunch	11:20	Lunch	12:00	Lunch
11:40	Math	12:00	Math	12:00	Math	12:40	Writing and conventions
12:50	Recess	12:50	Recess	12:50	Recess		
13:10	Social studies and science, with decoding pullout	13:10	Writing and conventions, with decoding pullout	13:10	Social studies, science, read aloud, and shared reading	13:35	Social studies and science, with decoding pullout
14:05	ELD support	14:05	ELD support	14:05	ELD support	14:05	ELD support

at least every other month or when a change in tier is considered. At any time in the process, referral for formal evaluation can begin if parents and staff feel it is necessary. (See page 203 for a reproducible Individualized Learning Plan form.)

Tier 3

When progress monitoring reveals that a student is not responding to Tier 1 and Tier 2 supports, R.H. Dana provides more intensive support. For example, a third-grade student whose reading difficulties are more severe may receive targeted phonics and fluency supports in addition to developmentally appropriate comprehension assistance. These more intensive supports may need to occur in place of social studies, science, or writing. R.H. Dana has decided that until students are reading at grade level, reading must take priority over these other important content areas. Tier 3 supports also occur in the reading room with students from various classrooms and grade levels with similar needs using targeted, scientifically based programs taught by highly trained interventionists.

The schedule of the interventionists is critical. Using Title I funds, Title III funds, other site funds, and special education personnel in a creative manner, pullouts can take place throughout the day. Each section or period of intervention lasts from 25–30 minutes. A schedule of all interventionists is shown in Table 11-2 (page 151).

Interventionists have time scheduled into their teaching day for progress monitoring, a task shared by the principal. The interventionists also have time scheduled into their day to support upper-grade classes with writing. While the school sees the need to intervene systematically in the area of mathematics, support in this content area is currently limited to regular, mandatory support during recesses for students below grade level in computational fluency.

R. H. Dana Elementary School is committed to doing whatever it takes to help students master literacy skills. By systematically and persistently diagnosing needs and prescribing targeted interventions, students are effectively supported in Tiers 1, 2, and 3.

Table 11-2: Interventionist Schedule at R. H. Dana Elementary School

	Reading Specialist	Full-Time Substitute	Full-Time Substitute	Instructional Aide	Resource Specialist	Resource Aide
7:45	Progress monitoring	Progress monitoring	Progress monitoring	Progress monitoring		
8:10	Comprehension, fluency, and vocabulary/language to first, second, and third graders	Comprehension, fluency, and decoding to third and fifth graders Fifth-grade writing support	Comprehension, fluency, and decoding to second and fourth graders Fourth-grade writing support	Fluency and vocabulary/language to second and third graders	Direct services as outlined in IEPs	Direct services as outlined in IEPs
11:30	Lunch					
12:00	Progress monitoring	Decoding to kindergarten students and first and fifth graders	Decoding to second and fourth graders		Decoding to kindergarten students	Comprehension and decoding to fourth and fifth graders

Pioneer Middle School

Pioneer Middle School in Tustin, California serves 1,300 students in grades 6–8. In 2004, its staff committed to a singular mission: to maximize *every* student's academic potential and personal responsibility.

To help fulfill this mission, Pioneer's staff developed a highly effective PRTI (see Figure 11-1, page 153).

Tier 1

The staff at Pioneer began by evaluating their Tier 1 core program, with a goal of making it firmly grounded in research-based best practices. To this end, the staff designed a weekly late-start schedule in which school starts 1 hour later every Wednesday to provide subject-based teacher teams with weekly collaboration time. Each department uses this time to identify essential learning standards, examples of rigor, academic vocabulary, and prerequisite skills that students need for every course of study. All courses are designed to meet or exceed state grade-level standards, thus ensuring that all students have access to high levels of learning. In addition, each team creates common assessments to measure student learning of each essential standard.

To provide all students with additional time and support, Pioneer has created the following Tier 1 programs:

- Open and closed tutorial periods

- Lunch or after-school help

- Sixth-grade mentors

- Study skills class

- Online grade access

Open and closed tutorial period. Every Tuesday and Thursday, Pioneer offers a tutorial period; teachers determine each week what they need to offer. Options include homework and assignment help, tutoring, make-up testing, reteaching of specific standards and skills, and enrichment activities. Most sessions are classified as open—any student may attend. Teachers also may require some students to attend a closed tutorial available only to assigned students. To mandate a student to attend, each teacher has a stamp that says "tutorial required," which is marked in the student's school planner on the day that he or she must go to this intervention.

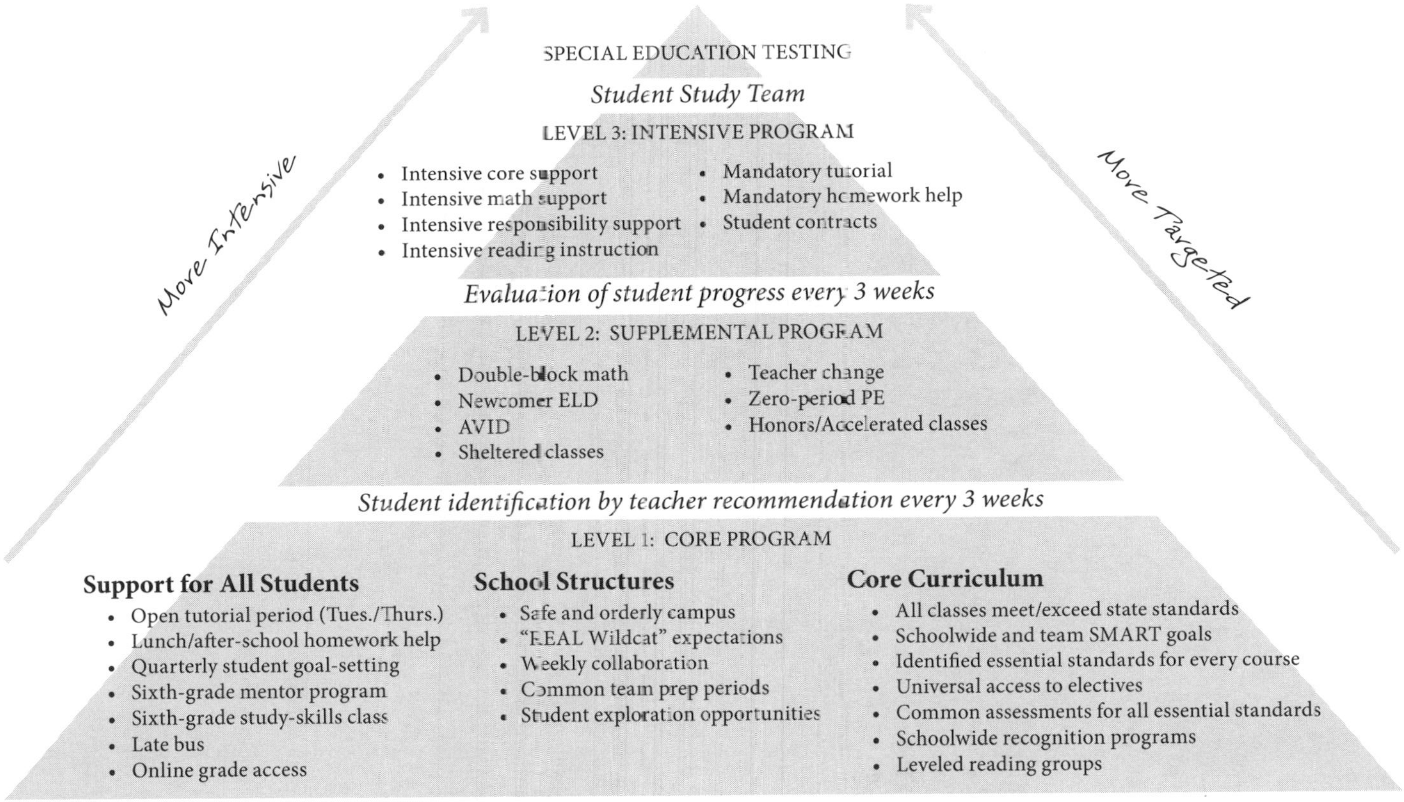

More Targeted

Move Intensive

SPECIAL EDUCATION TESTING

Student Study Team

LEVEL 3: INTENSIVE PROGRAM

- Intensive core support
- Intensive math support
- Intensive responsibility support
- Intensive reading instruction

- Mandatory tutorial
- Mandatory homework help
- Student contracts

Evaluation of student progress every 3 weeks

LEVEL 2: SUPPLEMENTAL PROGRAM

- Double-block math
- Newcomer ELD
- AVID
- Sheltered classes

- Teacher change
- Zero-period PE
- Honors/Accelerated classes

Student identification by teacher recommendation every 3 weeks

LEVEL 1: CORE PROGRAM

School Structures

- Safe and orderly campus
- "FEAL Wildcat" expectations
- Weekly collaboration
- Common team prep periods
- Student exploration opportunities

Core Curriculum

- All classes meet/exceed state standards
- Schoolwide and team SMART goals
- Identified essential standards for every course
- Universal access to electives
- Common assessments for all essential standards
- Schoolwide recognition programs
- Leveled reading groups

Support for All Students

- Open tutorial period (Tues./Thurs.)
- Lunch/after-school homework help
- Quarterly student goal-setting
- Sixth-grade mentor program
- Sixth-grade study-skills class
- Late bus
- Online grade access

Figure 11-1: Pioneer Middle School's pyramid response to intervention

Lunch or after-school homework help. Pioneer also offers lunchtime and after-school homework help. Sessions are subject-specific, with more than 20 offered per week. Homework help is open to all students, and to make sure that all students can take advantage of the after-school assistance, Pioneer offers a late bus every school day.

Sixth-grade mentors. The school assigns to every sixth-grade student an eighth-grade student, who serves as his or her mentor for the entire year. Each mentor works with a group of six to eight students. During weekly meetings, the mentor leads discussions and activities regarding transitioning into middle school, establishing good work habits, getting involved in extracurricular activities, setting goals, obtaining extra help, and understanding what it means to be a "Wildcat."

Study-skills class. Every sixth-grade student also participates in a 9-week study-skills class that teaches note-taking skills, studying techniques, and strategies for getting better organized.

Online grade access. A school that wants students to learn how to take responsibility for their academic achievement must give them access to their assignments and grades. To this end, every student has a personalized access code to review this information, as do his or her parents. Teachers update student grades at least once every 3 weeks.

Tier 2

Generally, mandatory tutorial and homework help are most effective for intentional nonlearners and for failed learners who need a little bit of extra guidance and practice with new learning skills. For failed learners that need more targeted and frequent supplemental support, Pioneer offers:

- Mandatory tutorial
- Mandatory homework help
- Students-at-risk conferences
- One-on-one mentor
- Double-block algebra and prealgebra
- Newcomer English-language development (ELD)
- Sheltered classes
- Advancement Via Individual Determination (AVID®)

- Change of teachers

Mandatory tutorial. While Pioneer's weekly tutorial periods are open to everyone, students referred into the school's intervention program must attend weekly tutorial sessions. Students are assigned to area(s) of need based on teacher referrals.

Mandatory homework help. Targeted students are required to attend homework-help sessions, which are offered before or after school, or during lunch.

Students-at-risk conferences. Pioneer holds a parent-teacher-student conference for each student who is in danger of retention or who fails to respond to interventions. All of the child's teachers attend, and conference participants develop an improvement plan for the child.

One-on-one mentor. The school assigns one-on-one peer mentors to targeted students. Mentors provide academic tutoring and/or assist in helping children understand social issues, such as difficulty making friends. Before serving as peer tutors, students receive training in an elective class.

Double-block algebra and prealgebra. Double-block math classes, which are for failed learners, last two periods and cover the same curriculum, scope, sequence, and timeline as the equivalent one-period, grade-level math class. The additional time provides the teacher the opportunity to utilize more hands-on and cooperative instructional practices; it also helps educators teach prerequisite skills for the next unit and provide other support for students to master essential material.

Newcomer English-language development. This class provides intensive ELD for students who are at the beginning levels of English acquisition. Instructors teach targeted academic vocabulary in science, social studies, and mathematics.

Sheltered classes. Staff assigns clusters of English-language learners (ELL) with similar needs to science, language arts, and social studies classes, which are led by teachers trained to use ELL instructional practices. In addition, peer tutors who speak the cluster students' native language assist them in this class.

Advancement Via Individual Determination (AVID). AVID is a college-focused elective course designed to support targeted students' access to rigorous coursework. This class teaches students study skills, as well as college and career planning, and also provides tutorial support to students in a college-prep curriculum.

Change of teachers. At times, some students struggle in a class because the teacher's instruction skills or attitudes are not well-suited for a particular student's needs. In this situation, the child can benefit from changing teachers.

To ensure that referred students attend their assigned interventions, they are required to record each session on an "Intervention Recording Chart" in their school-issued "Binder Reminder." The recorded information includes the date the student attended the intervention, the location, the assignment(s) completed, and the signature of the supervising staff member. A child's intervention coordinator checks the recording chart weekly. A student who consistently fails to attend his or her intervention sessions is assigned to escorted homework help, in which a staff member picks up the student from class and walks him or her to the assigned intervention.

To encourage family support and communication, the school provides progress reports of their children's current academic progress and area(s) of concern, with information on the current plan of intervention, to all parents and guardians of students referred into Pioneer's PRTI. Once a quarter, the school also invites parents and guardians to an information night on intervention programs and informs them of steps they can take to support their child's success.

Additionally, because Pioneer wants to maximize every student's academic potential, it offers an extensive accelerated course of study in math, language arts, social studies, and science. The staff regularly identifies students who have demonstrated mastery of grade-level essential standards in college prep classes and recommends these students for placement in honors-level coursework. Specific tutorial and homework assistance sessions are designed to help these students to make the jump to a more rigorous curriculum.

Table 11-3 (pages 157–159) summarizes Pioneer's Tier 2 interventions.

Table 11-3: Pioneer Middle School's Tier 2 Interventions

Intervention	Targeted Students	Intensity	Contract Requirements
Mandatory tutorial Targeted students must attend weekly tutorial sessions in areas of need, based on teacher referral.	Failed learners and intentional nonlearners in all subjects	Twice weekly, approximately 30 minutes per session	Instructors promote students from the intervention once all their grades are satisfactory.
Mandatory homework help Targeted students must attend lunch and/or after-school homework help sessions.	Intentional nonlearners, all subjects	1–10 times per week, depending on need Lunch homework help—25 minutes daily After-school homework help—60 minutes daily	Instructors promote students from the intervention once all their grades are satisfactory, based upon teacher's referral process.
Homework help sessions Staff members escort targeted students to assigned lunch and/or after-school homework help sessions.	Students who fail to attend assigned mandatory support	1–10 times per week, depending on need	Instructors promote students from the intervention once they demonstrate the ability to attend their assigned interventions independently.
Parent contact/ progress reports School contacts the parent(s) or guardian(s) of every student referred to the PRTI and provides a report of the child's academic progress and teachers' area(s) of concern.	All students referred to the PRTI	Every 3–4 weeks	Instructors promote students from the intervention once their grades are satisfactory, based upon the teacher referral process.
Fall and spring conferences for students at risk Parent-teacher-student conferences for students in danger of retention and/or of failing to respond to interventions. Participants create an improvement plan for the student.	Students at risk of retention or of failing to respond to interventions	Twice (October and March) per school year	Instructors promote students from this intervention once the children succeed in other Tier 2 interventions.

Table continues on page 158→

Intervention	Targeted Students	Intensity	Contract Requirements
One-on-one mentor School assigns one-on-one student mentor to targeted students. Mentor can provide academic peer-tutoring and/or help the targeted student learn how to gain peer acceptance.	Failed learners, intentional nonlearners, and other students with concerns about relating to peers	As needed	Teachers promote students upon successful remediation of the targeted concern.
Double-block math classes Two-period math class that meets the same curriculum, scope, sequence, and timeline as the equivalent one-period class. Additional time provides the teacher opportunity to utilize different instructional practices and teach prerequisite skills, and also provides additional support to help students master essential standards.	Failed learners in math	Daily, two periods	Teachers promote students when they perform successfully in the equivalent one-period course.
Newcomer English-language development (ELD) Class provides intensive ELD to targeted students.	Students lacking fluency in conversational English	Daily, three periods	Instructors promote students from the class when they demonstrate the English proficiency needed to be successful in the equivalent general education course.
Advancement Via Individual Determination (AVID) AVID is a college-focused elective course designed to support targeted students' access to rigorous coursework. Class teaches college and career planning, study skills, and offers tutorial support of college-prep curriculum.	Students with high ability who are low achieving	Daily, one period	N/A

Table continues on page 159→

Intervention	Targeted Students	Intensity	Contract Requirements
Sheltered classes Staff assigns students with similar language English-language learning (ELL) needs to science and/or core classes. Teacher is trained to use ELL instructional practices. Peer tutors who speak the cluster students' native language assist in the class.	ELL students who have graduated from the newcomer ELL class	Daily, one to three periods, as needed	Teachers promote students from the class once they demonstrate the level of English proficiency needed to be successful in the equivalent general education course.
Change of teachers Staff assigns targeted student to same course with a different teacher because present teaching style does not serve child's needs.	Students in need of a different instructional style and/or a new start	As needed	N/A
Zero-Period physical education (PE) Students assigned to mandatory, academic support electives and/or double-block math classes qualify to take their required PE class before school, thus allowing them to take an elective.	Students in a mandatory, academic support class and/or double-block math	As needed	Teachers promote students when staff no longer assign them to mandatory elective and/or double block math.
Honors classes Students can take honors classes in math, core subjects, and science.	Students who have demonstrated advanced mastery of grade-level essential standards	Each semester	N/A

Tier 3

While Pioneer's base and supplemental tiers meet the needs of the vast majority of students, a small minority of failed learners and intentional nonlearners need even more targeted and intensive interventions. To this end, Pioneer has created the following Tier 3 intensive interventions:

- Intensive core support (ICS)

- Intensive math support (IMS)

- Intensive reading instruction (IRI)

- Intensive responsibility support (IRS)

Intensive core support. ICS is a mandatory course designed to help targeted students to succeed in their grade-level core classes in language arts and social studies. The ICS instructor preteaches core essential material, reviews prerequisite skills children need to master these standards, and provides extended time for students to learn them. But this course does not replace the students' grade-level classes in language arts and social studies classes. Rather, it provides additional time and support for children to meet grade-level standards and to demonstrate an ability to learn future core standards without intensive support. When the child reaches this level, he or she is promoted from the class.

Intensive math support. IMS is an elective course that is made mandatory for targeted students who experience difficulties in grade-level math learning. The instructor preteaches essential grade-level math standards, reviews prerequisite skills needed to master these standards, and provides extended time for children to learn them.

Intensive reading instruction. IRI is another elective course that is made mandatory for targeted students to help them achieve reading proficiency to grade level. Here too, instructors preteach core essential standards, review prerequisite skills needed to master them, and provide additional time for students to learn them. To be promoted from the class, students must demonstrate the ability to read at or above grade level.

Intensive responsibility support. IRS is an elective course that is made mandatory for intentional nonlearners to require them to complete all assignments and to demonstrate effective study skills. The students' classroom teachers provide the IRS instructor all of the child's missing assignments. To be promoted from the class, students must have received a least a 70% grade in all classes, complete all assignments, record assignments properly for at least 3 weeks, and demonstrate satisfactory attendance.

Table 11-4 (page 161) summarizes Pioneer's Tier 3 interventions. Tier 3 students can also continue to receive any of the Tier 2 interventions, such as mandatory tutorial and mandatory homework help. In addition, the school holds a parent-student conference for every student placed in an intensive support class. At the meeting, the student signs a contract that details his or her learning goals, the support that the school will provide,

Table 11-4: Pioneer Middle School's Tier 3 Interventions

Intervention	Targeted Students	Intensity	Contract Requirements
Intensive core support (ICS) Instructor focus is preteaching core essential standards, reviewing prerequisite skills needed to master them, and providing extended time to learn them.	Failed learners in language arts and social studies	Daily, one period	Instructors promote students when they demonstrate mastery of grade-level core essential standards, as well as the ability to learn future core essential standards without intensive support.
Intensive math support (IMS) Instructor focus is on preteaching grade-level math essential standards, reviewing prerequisite skills needed to master grade-level essential standards, and providing extended time for students to learn grade-level math essential standards.	Failed learners in math	Daily, one period	Instructors promote students when they demonstrate mastery of grade-level core essential standards, as well as the ability to learn future core essential standards without intensive support.
Intensive reading instruction (IRI) This mandatory course is designed to increase targeted students' reading proficiency to grade level. Instructor focus is preteaching core essential standards, reviewing prerequisite skills needed to master them, and providing extended time to learn core essential standards.	Failed learners who read at least 2 years below grade level	Daily, one period	Instructors promote students who demonstrate ability to read at or above grade level.
Intensive responsibility support (IRS) This mandatory course is designed to require intentional nonlearners to complete all assignments and to demonstrate effective study skills.	Intentional nonlearners	Daily, one period	Instructors promote students who have at least a 70% in all classes and who have completed all assignments, recorded them properly for at least 3 weeks, and completed all assignments throughout the intervention.

the child's responsibilities, and the requirements that the child must meet to be promoted from the program.

Because Pioneer believes that students assigned to interventions still should be able to retain their elective classes, children in mandatory academic support or double-block math classes may take their required physical education classes before school, thus allowing them to select an elective and so explore new interests. In addition, except for Pioneer's after-school homework help sessions, the site offers each intervention during the school day, which guarantees that all interventions are available for all students.

If a student fails to respond to Pioneer's Tiers 1, 2, and 3, then a student study team considers sending the child for special education testing. Based upon the results of these tests, an individualized plan of core instruction and intervention supports is designed and implemented.

The Referral Process

Pioneer's student identification process begins with universal screening of all students in reading, writing, and mathematics. These tests are administered the first week of school, at the end of the first semester, and at the end of the school year. Not only does this information help identify students who may need additional time and support, but it provides critical information on the effectiveness of our core program, as these tests measure growth of all students. Additionally, the administration meets with every "feeder" elementary school to explain the school's intervention programs and ask fifth-grade teachers to identify students who may need additional help.

Once the school year starts, every 3 weeks, all teachers recommend students in their classes who need additional support. The teachers refer students electronically, utilizing the same technology with which they send quarterly grades. As part of the process, teachers register each student's current academic grade and work habits.

The teacher referrals are compiled in the office, and a counselor or administrator is assigned to each referred student to serve as his or her intervention coordinator. These coordinators work with a particular class of students for all three years at Pioneer; for example, the sixth-grade intervention coordinator will follow his or her students in the seventh and eighth grades, thus developing a strong relationship with specific children who need ongoing support. Throughout the entire process, the intervention coordinator keeps written records on each student, recording his or her participation in interventions and progress made in learning new skills. This information is also recorded electronically in the school's student database.

After the school has utilized some or all of the options to help a failing student, a student study team meets to review the impact of these efforts taken and to consider special education testing. Cognitive and achievement assessments may provide the team with a depth of information to better determine why the student is struggling and what additional steps can be taken.

Whittier Union High School District

The Whittier Union High School District in southern California is comprised of five comprehensive high schools, one continuation high school, one independent study high school, and one adult school, enrolling a total of more than 13,700 students. Approximately 45% of the district's students are part of the free and reduced lunch program, and approximately 13% are English-language learners.

The district and all of its high schools have spent considerable time since 2004 working on changing the culture from one that reluctantly accepted the "fact" that some kids fail to one that believes that all kids can learn and that failure is not an option. Initially, the high schools began creating common assessments and using the data to find who was learning and who wasn't, as well as to better understand which students were having the greatest difficulties in learning. At this juncture, Whittier Union began to dig deeply into answering the question, "Now that we understand which kids need more time and support, and what they are having difficulty learning, what are we going to do about it?" Answering this question produced a number of changes in bell schedules and resulted in new programs and positions. More importantly, it changed the way the high schools thought about their basic mission, shifting their focus to learning, not just teaching.

Easing the Transition

Whittier Union high schools have initiated a number of programs focusing on their ninth-grade students, who come from nine middle schools in five different elementary school districts. Campus Watch is one of the programs they've initiated to ease the transition into high school. Modeled after the Counselor Watch program at Adlai Stevenson High School, Campus Watch involves the whole school, not just school counselors. The high schools solicited information from the feeder middle schools on students thought to be at risk, resulting in about 400 names in the program's first year. That number now exceeds 2,000 and has helped focus high school efforts on helping these students get off to a good start. Campus Watch has become so successful, in fact, that one of the high schools now asks for information on *every* student in order to better understand the needs of all students the moment they enter the high school. Whittier Union anticipates that this comprehensive screening of new high school students will become the Campus Watch model of the future.

All Whittier high schools organize a Freshman First Day, also based on a similar program at Stevenson High School. Freshmen start school a day early, allowing the staff to get them engaged in the life of the high school as early as possible by channeling them into clubs, school sports, and other cocurricular activities before school actually starts. Freshmen attend each of their classes, meet their teachers, and learn more about the opportunities and expectations of their new school. Freshman First Day helps new students make a strong personal connection to their new school and become successful "high schoolers" as early as possible.

Another component that has proven to be very successful in helping freshmen make the transition to high school is Link Crew, a program that welcomes freshmen and makes them feel comfortable throughout the first year of their high school experience. While this program is widely recognized and used throughout America, Whittier high schools have stood out by enlisting more and more of the Link Crew students to act as tutors in the classroom and as part of targeted interventions. Having an additional 100 high school students volunteer to serve as tutors speaks to a true cultural change—from "sifting and sorting," allowing some to fail—to ensuring that all students learn.

Much of this work is coordinated by a newly created position, the *intervention specialist,* a teacher who has two release periods in order to coordinate intervention services, and prepare and funnel information and test data to the appropriate staff members. In addition, each high school has identified 10–14 teachers who act as course leads, collecting and preparing data for collaborative team meetings for specific courses (such as Algebra I or English I) in order to better target the interventions. Course leads are paid a small stipend for their efforts and are often teachers interested in becoming administrators looking for additional leadership opportunities.

Expecting and Supporting Success

Whittier Union's shift in culture is evident in the fact that college preparation is the lowest "track" and Algebra I the lowest math course available at the high schools. To support their higher expectations, it became necessary to design and deliver powerful academic interventions through tutoring and other support programs. These tutoring programs have become increasingly more targeted as better assessment data becomes available. For example, tutoring for Algebra I focuses on procedural knowledge specific to individual students rather than simply being offered to students who "flunked Algebra I." These focused interventions are informed by student performance data from common assessments and other benchmark assessment results that have been reviewed in departmental professional learning community discussions.

For example, the high schools offer a guided study class patterned after Adlai Stevenson's program. Once the Campus Watch forms are returned from the feeder middle schools, certain students are automatically directed into a guided study class as their freshman elective. Each of the district's five high schools has designed this class a little bit differently to learn what works best for its own students, as well as to discover some best practices that might be shared among the five comprehensive high schools.

While many students exit this program at the semester or end of the freshman year, guided study is now being piloted for 10th-grade students as well. Anecdotally, guided study teachers reported that many of their previous students continued to "hang out" in the guided study classroom, which suggested that students continued to benefit from the environment. A review of student data revealed that some students still required additional time in a structured, supported environment after their freshman year, which confirmed the decision to enhance 10th-grade support. In all of Whittier Union's high schools, student placement in academic support occurs following each 4.5-week grading period. In an effort to provide even more timely and effective support, the district is exploring moving to 3-week grading periods.

One of the Whittier Union high schools, La Serna, has created a pyramid of interventions and modified its master schedule (visit go.solution-tree.com/rti to see the schedule) to provide a lunch schedule that is half lunch and half tutorial. These tutorials are regarded as classes—roll is taken—and students quickly learn that La Serna is closely monitoring their attendance and will respond promptly with consequences when they don't attend! These changes in bell schedule grew out of an understanding that inviting students to after-school or Saturday sessions simply doesn't work.

Serving the Students Most at Risk

The next tier of Whittier's pyramid of preventions/interventions includes high intensity, more individualized interventions for those students still struggling to achieve academic success. Many students, especially students with disabilities, enter high school unable to read well enough to access the high school curriculum. These students perform poorly, dislike school, and often do not graduate. The district special education team took on the challenge of developing an intensive intervention to support special education students in improving this critical foundational skill as soon as they entered high school.

Beginning in 2006–07, *all* incoming ninth-grade special education students identified as reading at the third- or fourth-grade level were enrolled in a reading class (as their elective) that uses the Pearson AMP Reading System. Each class is limited to 15 students and is taught by a special education teacher trained to teach AMP and committed to implementing the program with fidelity. Meetings with program teachers were held throughout the school year to ensure fidelity of implementation and provide support as needed.

The most important measure of the success of any instructional support program is student progress towards graduation. In an evaluation of the academic performance of this first group of students in the AMP program at the end of their first semester of 10th grade, 90% of AMP students had earned a C or better in their core curriculum courses. Many students experienced consistent academic success for the first time. As the program continues, the district will also utilize performance on the California High School Exit Examination (CAHSEE) as an additional measure.

For those 12th-grade students who, despite numerous attempts and other interventions, have not yet passed the CAHSEE in English language arts and/or mathematics (required to earn a diploma in California), Whittier has taken an even more intensive and directed approach. These students are enrolled in a focused support program based on Measuring Up, a research-based supplemental instructional program aligned to state curriculum standards and the CAHSEE. This program, offered each period of the day at the high schools, is delivered by teachers hired specifically for the program as well as by student tutors. Students receive intensive, individualized support with online access at school and from home. Frequent prescriptive assessment allows students to concentrate on areas of greatest need and informs teachers on the effectiveness of their daily instruction. In an extraordinary demonstration of a culture of commitment to student success, teachers of elective courses have agreed to excuse targeted students from their course during the weeks of instruction prior to the next administration of the CAHSEE and then reinstate the students into their elective after taking the CAHSEE.

Previously, very few of these 12th-grade students at high risk passed the CAHSEE. While traditional interventions had been tried repeatedly and failed, Measuring Up has proven very successful. During the 2006-07 school year, 99.4% of all seniors in the Whittier Union High School District passed the CAHSEE. Because of the individualized, customized services provided to students at risk, many more of them are now earning their high school diplomas.

Rising to the Challenge

These schools, like many in America today, are faced with changing demographics, declining budgets, and increased expectations. But rather than continuing to focus on the shortcomings of their students, parents, or communities, these educators have risen to the challenge by implementing new programs and schedules to provide additional time and support to students when they don't learn. Most importantly, they have undertaken the more difficult yet more rewarding task of changing the structure of their schools—of seeing what they do through new eyes.

Now that you have created a schoolwide, systematic PRTI, how will you begin implementation?

See page 195 for "PRTI Critical Steps to Success," a graphic organizer to help your team synthesize the information from previous activities and identify 4–8 critical first steps.

See page 197 for "PRTI Essential Standard Plan," an organization chart to help your team plan a PRTI process to ensure that your students will master a targeted essential standard. The chart addresses all the critical elements of PRTI.

See page 200 for "Creating a PRTI." Using a pyramid graphic, this culminating activity will help your team create a visual that represents your schoolwide PRTI.

Visit **go.solution-tree.com/rti**
to download these activities.

Epilogue

A Moral Responsibility

The price of greatness is responsibility.

—Winston Churchill

As we stated in the opening chapter, this book was written by practitioners for practitioners. Our goal has been to provide our fellow educators with a powerful, research-based, highly effective process to ensure high levels of learning for all students. We have offered a compelling case for a pyramid response to intervention, demonstrated how PRTI's guiding principles and procedures are firmly grounded in research-based best practices, described the entire PRTI process in detail, and provided real-life examples. We know this process works because we have successfully implemented PRTI practices at the site and district levels, at elementary and secondary schools, at small and large schools, at rural and urban schools, and at schools that range from highly affluent, native English-speaking students to schools with high rates of economically disadvantaged, English-language learning students. In every case, the results on student achievement have been substantial, significant, and sustainable.

Having been provided with the knowledge and skills needed to effectively respond when students don't learn, only one question remains: Are you willing to do the hard work necessary to make these outcomes a reality for your students? Our experience tells us that successful implementation depends greatly upon a staff's collective motivations and convictions for starting down this path. If the cause is considered noble and the goal is perceived achievable, a vast majority of educators will be willing to work tirelessly to accomplish the collective good. But if the cause is considered undistinguished or the goal is perceived as unobtainable, then creating the collective vision and commitment needed to succeed is virtually impossible. For this reason, we caution schools that commence with this vital work as a means to improve test scores, or because the state or district has mandated them to do so. Such calls to action hardly inspire, for none of us became educators because it was our life's ambition to raise test scores or meet "average" yearly progress. Individuals rarely work passionately to implement what they are forced to do; there is no better example of this than the mandates dictated by No Child Left Behind. Even worse, such misguided priorities can distract our thinking away from processes that help all students learn and instead toward intervention decisions such as focusing school efforts on "bubble kids" who are just below proficient. Such thinking is contradictory to the underlying values of a learning-focused school and can ultimately lead to practices that are counterproductive to a PRTI. This is not to suggest that a PRTI will not raise test scores—improvement in standardized assessments will occur as a natural outcome when schools focus on all students learning at higher levels.

If raising test scores or meeting external mandates are not the primary purposes for creating a site PRTI, then what should compel our efforts? The answer to this question lies in why we joined this profession in the first place—to help children. There is no more powerful engine for change than a group of educators who have collectively taken responsibility for their students' success. Our work must be driven by the knowledge that our collaborative efforts will determine the lifelong success or life-ending failure of our students. Building a PRTI should not be a program to raise student test scores, but rather a process to realize children's hopes and dreams; it should not be a way to meet state mandates, but a means to serve humanity. Once we understand the urgency of our work and embrace this noble cause as our fundamental purpose, how could we possibly allow any child to fail?

Appendix

Reproducibles

Visit **go.solution-tree.com/rti** to download these
reproducibles and other helpful information.

How Do Our School's Current Practices Align With the Essential Elements of RTI?

Essential Element of RTI	Our Current Reality	Our Desired Outcome (Long-Term Goal)	Our First Steps (Short-Term Goal)
Have we embraced that RTI is not a special education or regular education program, but rather a schoolwide process that requires collective responsibility to ensure that all students learn?			
Is our instructional program standards-based and research-based?			
Is our instructional program delivered with fidelity by highly qualified teachers?			
Do we universally screen all students with comprehensive literacy and mathematics assessments several times a year?			
Do we frequently progress monitor students at risk in all tiers?			
Do we know when to provide students more intensive support?			
Do we communicate regularly with parents and other stakeholders?			

How Will Our School Respond to Key RTI Questions?

Key Questions of RTI	Our Current Reality	Our Desired Outcome (Long-Term Goal)	Our First Steps (Short-Term Goal)
How many tiers of intervention can our school provide?			
How will our school identify students in need of support?			
Will our school employ the problem-solving approach, the protocol approach, or a blended approach?			
How will we define what determines an *adequate* response to intervention?			
What is the function of special education when implementing RTI?			

What Elements of RTI Are Present in the Pioneering Models?

Model Program	Schoolwide Culture	Strengthened Tier 1	Universal Screening	Tier 2 Supplemental Interventions	Progress Monitoring	Tier 3 Intensive Interventions	Decision Protocols	Communication to Stakeholders
TLC								
ExCEL								
CAST								
HAEA								
Washington								

Creating a PLC Foundation

Potential Bump	Essential Question(s)	Our Current Reality	Our Desired Outcome (Long-Term Goal)	Our First Steps (Short-Term Goal)
Big Idea #1: A Focus on Learning	Do we believe all students can learn at high levels? Will we take responsibility to make this a reality?			
Big Idea #2: Collaborative Culture	How often do our collaborative teams meet? Is the collaboration time during the teachers' professional day? Is it required?			
Norms	Has each team identified team norms? Are they reviewed at every meeting? Is there a "norm check" procedure?			
What do we want our students to learn?	Have collaborative teams clearly defined essential learning outcomes?			
Big Idea #3: A Focus on Results	Have collaborative teams created common assessments to measure essential standards?			
How will we know if our students are learning?	Do the assessment results show how each student did on individual essential standards? Is common assessment data shared in comparison to others?			
START!	What can we start doing tomorrow that will move our school closer to our PLC goals? What obstacles must we address?			

Creating a Learning Mission

Recall the two fundamental assumptions undergirding a school's mission to provide high levels of learning for all students: 1) Educators believe that all students are capable of high levels of learning, and 2) they assume the responsibility to make this outcome a reality for every child. This exercise offers a process to create a common mission of learning.

Step 1: Create Individual Mission Statements

Have staff members sit in teams. Ask each person to write a response in 8 to 12 words to the question, "What is the fundamental purpose (mission) of our school? In other words, why does our school exist?"

Step 2: Share Individual Mission Statements

Ask each person to share his or her answer and ask a team member to chart the responses. Once all team members have shared, have each team discuss how the responses are similar and how they are different. Then inquire, "How can we work collaboratively to help our students if we have different missions for our school?"

Step 3: Create Team Mission Statements

Have each team create a collective mission statement in 8 to 12 words. The purpose is not to combine all the ideas into a comprehensive "laundry list," but rather to find consensus on your school's single most important purpose.

Step 4: Share Team Mission Statements

Ask each team to share its mission statement with the entire group and chart the answers. Ask, "How are our responses similar? How are they different?"

Step 5: Create a School Mission Statement

Using the team statements as a resource, create a collective mission statement of 8 to 12 words for your school. Again, reach consensus on the single most important purpose of your school and do not combine all the ideas or make a laundry list.

Step 6: Check Alignment

In a PLC, the fundamental purpose of a school must be learning. It is not a school's mission to ensure that all students are taught, but rather that all students learn. To this end, ask, "Does our final school mission embrace learning?"

Identifying Essential Standards

A school cannot create an effective site intervention if it has not clearly defined the essential learning outcomes of each grade, subject, and course of study. This exercise helps a team answer, "What is it we expect students to learn?"

Grade Level: _____ Subject: _____ Team Members: _____

Standard #	Standard/Description	Example/Rigor	Prior Skills Needed	Common Assessment	When Taught?

continued on page 178↓

Sample Essential Standards: Algebra 1

Standard #	Standard/Description	Example/Rigor	Prior Skills Needed	Common Assessment	When Taught?
2.0 10.0	Students understand and use the rules of exponents. Students multiply and divide monomials.	Simplify: $\dfrac{5x3\ y7}{10xy9}$	Multiplying monomials and polynomials (Chapter 4)	Chapter 4 CA	Feb.
11.0	Students apply basic factoring techniques to second-and simple third-degree polynomials. These techniques include finding a common factor for all terms in a polynomial, recognizing the difference of two squares, and recognizing perfect squares of binomials.	Factor completely: 1. 3a2 – 24ab + 48b2 2. x2 – 121 3. 9x2 + 12x +4	Multiplying and dividing monomials and polynomials (Chapter 4 and Chapter 5: Sec 1–3)	Chapter 5 CA	Feb.
12.0	Students simplify fractions with polynomials in the numerator and denominator by factoring both and reducing them to the lowest terms.	Simplify: $\dfrac{x^2-4xy+4y^2}{3xy-6y^2}$	Factoring by finding the greatest common factor, difference of two squares, and trinomials (Chapter 5)	Chapter 6 CA	March
2.0	Students understand and use the operation of taking a root and raising to a fractional power.	Simplify: $\sqrt{16}+\sqrt[3]{8}$	Understanding rational and irrational numbers and prime factoring	Chapter 11: Sec 3–5 CA	March
14.0	Solve a quadratic equation by factoring or completing the square.	Solve by completing the square: x² + 4x = 6	Factor quadratics (Chapter 5) and simplifying radicals (Chapter 11)	Chapter 12: Sec 1–4 and Chapter 5 Sec 12 CA	Late March
21.0	Students graph quadratic functions and know that their roots are the x-intercepts.	Graph: y = x² – 3x – 4 and state the x-intercepts.	Solving quadratic equations by factoring, completing the square, and using quadratic formula (Chapter 12)	Chapter 8: Sec 8 and p. 389 CA	April

continued on page 179

Sample Essential Standards: U.S. History

Standard #	Standard/Description	Example/Rigor	Prior Skills Needed	Common Assessment	When Taught?
8.1.1	Describe the relationships between the moral/political ideas of the Great Awakening & the Enlightenment and the development of revolutionary fervor.	*Prompt* Describe how the movements GA/E led to the development of revolutionary fervor	*Define & Understand* The Great Awakening Enlightenment	*Venn Diagram* Compare/contrast movements with written analysis.	1st Quarter: Sept. Resources: Chapter 2
8.1	Understand the major events preceding the American Revolution.		cause-and-effect relationships	*Timeline of Events* Illustrated & annotated	1st Quarter: Sept./Oct. Resources: Chapter 3
8.1.2	Analyze the philosophy of government expressed in the Declaration of Independence. (individual rights)	*Test Question* Which of the following is not an unalienable right?	7.6.5 Experience analyzing historical documents. (Magna Carta)	*Analysis of Primary Source Document* The Declaration of Independence Identification of key phrases "All men are created . . . " (unalienable rights)	1st Quarter: October Resources: Chapter 3
8.1.5	Understand the significance of religious freedom within the First Amendment and the importance of separation of church and state.	Why did the Supreme Court overturn *Tinker v. Des Moines?*	Understand the various elements of the 1st Amendment.	*1st Amendment Case Study* Research case, prepare visual, & present	1st Semester Nov.
8.2.7	Describe the principles of federalism, dual sovereignty, separation of powers, checks and balances, purpose of majority rule, and ideas of American constitutionalism.	How does the legislative branch check the executive branch?	Understand the three branches of government as well as the idea of checks and balances.	Constitution test	2nd Quarter

Unpacking the Standards

Robert Marzano notes that teachers cannot possibly cover all standards; instead, schools should prioritize them so that depth of learning results. This activity will help educators to translate content standards into essential pedagogic questions.

1. Prepare for the activity with staff.

   - Choose a content area.

   - Find released state test questions that are matched to standards for that content area.

   - Enlarge the test questions so they are more readable.

   - Write each standard number and language on the top of legal-sized paper. Legal-sized paper is preferable to butcher paper because it can be copied for distribution later.

   - Spread the legal-sized paper on desks in a classroom, and prepare teachers for the activity.

2. Direct the activity.

   - Ask teachers to cut and paste the released test questions on the sheet of legal-sized paper that represents the corresponding standard.

   - Have teachers analyze the released questions for each standard.

   - Request that teachers rewrite the standards in student-friendly language.

3. Follow up on the activity.

   - Copy the legal-sized papers (each should include one standard, its rewording in student-friendly language, and representative questions from released tests).

   - Distribute to each classroom teacher a packet that contains a complete set of state standards for that grade level's content area.

   - Suggest that each instructor use the packet as a resource for interpreting and mastering content standards in order to prepare students for state tests.

Common Formative Assessments (CFAs)

In an effective intervention program, teacher teams use assessment information to identify students who need additional time and support to master content, as well as to confirm which core instructional strategies most effectively meet their students' needs. In this exercise, which draws on the work of Larry Ainsworth and Donald Viegut (2006), a team can examine existing student assessment tools and review important considerations for creating measurements for learning.

It is first important to appreciate just what a common formative assessment is, and what it isn't. First, determine whether the assessment tools you employ or are planning to use meet the following criteria.

CFAs

- ☐ Assess higher order thinking
- ☐ Require application rather than recall of knowledge
- ☐ Assess learning in a new context
- ☐ Provide immediate feedback to the teacher and learner
- ☐ Give results in time to make meaningful instructional adjustments
- ☐ Actively motivate and involve students in the process
- ☐ Diagnose needs of individuals and classes
- ☐ Prescribe follow-up actions

- ☐ Are frequent, short assessments
- ☐ Are assessments for learning rather than assessments of learning
- ☐ Are teacher-created, not standardized tests
- ☐ Contain multiple types of problems
- ☐ Are collaboratively scored and analyzed
- ☐ Are based on power standards

Next, list all existing assessments currently in use and ask: Are they necessary? To what extent do they help diagnose student needs and inform future teaching and learning? These steps will almost certainly take more time than preparing student tests.

continued on page 182→

Common Formative Assessments (CFAs) (Cont'd)

Using this table, list all important assessments given during a year (on a scale of 1 to 5).

Assessments	Rank Based on Impact on Instruction and Student Learning (1 = greatest impact)	Rank Based on Alignment to Power Standards (1 = most aligned)

Next, fill out the following table.

Topic:			
List power standards (ideally, 2–3)	List essential learnings—the big ideas you want students to know	Write test questions (ideally, 3–4 per standard)	Create rubrics and answer keys for power standards

Adapted from Ainsworth, L, & Viegut, D. (2006). *Common formative assessments: How to connect standards-based instruction and assessment.* Thousand Oaks, CA: Corwin Press.

Common Assessment Desired Outcomes

Giving a common assessment is not an end in itself, but a means to better measure teaching and student learning. To this end, whenever your team reviews common assessment data, consider the following critical outcomes and essential questions to get the most out of your common assessments.

We give common assessments so we can . . .

. . . **Identify which students have not demonstrated mastery of essential standard(s).**
Because we give common assessments to measure student mastery of essential standard(s), common assessments should identify those students who need additional help and support. Additionally, if an assessment measures more than one essential standard, then the test results must provide more than an overall score for each student, but also delineate specifically which standards each student did not pass.

Essential Question: Which specific students did not demonstrate mastery?

. . . **Identify effective instructional practices.** Because our teachers have autonomy in how they teach essential standards, it is vital that common assessment data help validate which practices were effective. This can be done best when common assessment results are displayed in such a way that allows each teacher to compare his or her students' results to other teachers who teach the same course.

Essential Question: Which instructional practices proved to be most effective?

. . . **Identify patterns in student mistakes.** Besides using common assessment results to identify best instructional practices, this data should also be used to determine ineffective instructional practices. When analyzing the types of mistakes that failing students make, note patterns that point to weaknesses or gaps in the initial instruction.

Essential Question: What patterns can we identify from the student mistakes?

. . . **Measure the accuracy of the assessment.** Analyze the validity of each test question. Over time, this will build a team's capacity to create better assessments.

Essential Question: How can we improve this assessment?

. . . **Plan and target interventions: The ultimate goal of any professional learning community is to ensure high levels of learning for all students.** If your team uses common assessments to identify students in need of additional help, determine effective and ineffective instructional practices, and measure the validity of the assessment, you will have the information needed to plan and implement targeted interventions to assist the students that need help.

Essential Question: What interventions are needed to provide failed students additional time and support?

Who Are Our Under-Represented Students?

Under-Represented Student Group	Data Supporting Group as Under-Represented	Possible Underlying Causes for the Group's Under-Represented Status	Our First Steps (Short-Term Goal)

What Are Our Human and Fiscal Resources?

Personnel	Programs	Categorical (Restricted) Funds	Noncategorical Funds

Evaluating Our Current Interventions

A schoolwide, systematic PRTI is only as effective as the specific interventions that comprise it. With your team, follow these steps to evaluate your school's current and potential site interventions, using the chart on the next page to record your discussion.

1. Brainstorm a list of your school's current and proposed interventions.

2. Evaluate each current intervention's alignment with the essential characteristics of "Learning CPR":

   - *Urgent*—Do we have a sense of urgency when implementing this intervention?

   - *Directive*—Are targeted students "required" to attend or participate?

   - *Timely*—How often are students identified for this program? How often do we evaluate progress? Does this intervention provide extended learning time and multiple opportunities for students to demonstrate mastery?

   - *Targeted*—What is the intervention's intended outcome? Does it provide differentiated, research-based instruction? Which students should be selected for participation?

   - *Administered by Trained Professionals*—Who will teach or otherwise implement this intervention? Do our instructors have the training and resources necessary for success?

   - *Systematic*—How do we identify and provide support to all students who need this intervention? What criteria will we use to move students into and out of the program? How do we know whether the intervention is working?

3. Evaluate and revise or eliminate individual interventions if you deem them ineffective or unnecessary.

4. Create your pyramid response to intervention, using the program of highly effective interventions that you have identified or redesigned as your starting point.

continued on page 187→

Evaluating Our Current Interventions (Cont'd)

Intervention Focus	Program Strengths in Comparison to Essential Characteristics	Program Concerns in Comparison to Essential Characteristics	Desired Outcome	Alignment Steps

What Is Our Tier 1 Core Program?

Questions for Tier 1	Our Current Reality	Our Desired Outcome (Long-Term Goal)	Our First Steps (Short-Term Goal)
How do we provide all students access to grade-level essential standards?			
What evidence do we have that our Tier 1 or core practices are research-based?			
What assessments can we use to universally screen students several times a year so that no students fall through the cracks?			
How can we adjust our curricular and instructional practices to "shore up the core?"			
How can we provide a first dose of differentiated intervention in our Tier 1 core program?			
Does our Tier 1 core program meet the learning needs of at least 75–80% of our students?			

What Are Our Tier 2 Supplemental Interventions?

Questions for Tier 2	Our Current Reality	Our Desired Outcome (Long-Term Goal)	Our First Steps (Short-Term Goal)
Which Tier 2 interventions are targeted to help failed learners?			
Which Tier 2 interventions are targeted to help intentional nonlearners?			
How do we know that our interventions are research-based, implemented with fidelity, and administered by highly trained staff?			
What are our decision protocols for the identification and placement of students into Tier 2 interventions?			
How often will we monitor progress and revise student placement?			

What Are Our Tier 3 Intensive Interventions?

Questions for Tier 3	Our Current Reality	Our Desired Outcome (Long-Term Goal)	Our First Steps (Short-Term Goal)
Which Tier 3 interventions are targeted to help failed learners?			
Which Tier 3 interventions are targeted to help intentional nonlearners?			
How do we know that our interventions are research-based, implemented with fidelity, and administered by highly trained staff?			
What are our decision protocols for the identification and placement of students into Tier 3 interventions?			
How often will we monitor progress and revise student placement?			
What are our decision protocols for the referral of students to formal evaluation to determine special education eligibility?			

What Are Our Behavioral Interventions?

Questions for Behavioral Interventions	Our Current Reality	Our Desired Outcome (Long-Term Goal)	Our First Steps (Short-Term Goal)
How will we provide universal support for student behavior at Tier 1 that clearly defines expected behaviors as well as incentives and consequences?			
How will we provide Tier 2 interventions and supports that teach replacement behaviors to small groups of students?			
How will we provide Tier 3 interventions and supports that are 1) highly intensive and targeted for individual students and 2) prescribed based upon a behavioral assessment that identifies the antecedents to the undesirable behavior?			
How do we know that our interventions are research-based, implemented with fidelity, and administered by highly trained staff?			
What are our decision protocols for the identification and placement of students into behavioral interventions?			
How often will we monitor progress and revise student placement?			

Functional Behavior Analysis Protocol

Problem	Give a specific example of the problem.	What would we actually see the student doing in class?	If there is more than one problem, with which problem should we begin?
Complexity	What other factors are involved?	In what other settings does this behavior occur?	Has there recently been a change in the frequency or duration of the behavior?
Analysis	What happens just before the problem occurs?	What happens just after the behavior occurs?	How do other students react to the behavior?

continued on page 193↓

Functional Behavior Analysis Protocol (Cont'd)

Replacement Behavior	What are we asking the student to do when the problem behavior occurs?	Is the student already demonstrating some replacement behaviors? What? When?	What level of progress will you find to be acceptable?
Measurement	When during the day would we get the best picture of the problem?	How long should we measure the problem? For an entire day, part of a day, or part of a period?	How will we measure the behavior? By number of incidents, duration, intensity, or all three factors?
Current Status	What have we done already in response to the behavior?	Have some things worked briefly?	How have we dealt with similar problems in the past?

How Will We Coordinate, Document, and Communicate About Our PRTI?

Key Questions	Our Current Reality	Our Desired Outcome (Long-Term Goal)	Our First Steps (Short-Term Goal)
How will we communicate our intervention program to students and parents?			
How will we document what we have done and how it has affected student progress?			
What is our decision protocol for referral to more intensive tiers and to special education?			

PRTI Critical Steps to Success

There are four broad, critical areas of focus that must be considered when creating a PRTI:

1. Align school culture and structures to the "3 Big Ideas" of being a PLC.

2. Implement the critical elements of RTI.

3. Align site interventions to "Learning CPR."

4. Create a process to universally screen, identify, place, and monitor students who need additional time and support.

It is important to remember that each of these areas are essential aspects of a PRTI and must be implemented simultaneously to create an effective PRTI. At the same time, considering all four at the same time can be overwhelming. The graphic organizer on page 196 will help your team identify manageable first steps. The process is as follows.

1. Professional Learning Communities: Using the "First Steps" identified from the activity "Creating a PLC Foundation" (page 175), discuss and prioritize these actions. Next, transfer these steps below the corresponding "Big Idea" in area #1 of the PRTI Critical Steps to Success Chart.

2. Response to Intervention: Using the "First Steps" identified from the activity "How Do Our School's Current Practices Align With the Essential Elements of RTI?" (page 172), discuss and prioritize these actions. Next, transfer these steps below the corresponding critical element in area #2 of the PRTI Critical Steps to Success Chart.

3. Learning CPR: Review the interventions that were listed and revised on the activity "Evaluating Our Current Interventions" (page 186). Which intervention would have the greatest impact and leverage at Tier 2? At Tier 3? For intentional nonlearners? For failed learners? Next, transfer these interventions to area #3 of the PRTI Critical Steps to Success Chart.

4. Identify, Place, and Monitor Students: Review the identification, placement, and monitoring processes addressed in the activities, "What Is Our Tier 1 Core Program?" (page 188), "What Are Our Tier 2 Supplemental Interventions?" (page 189), and "What Are Our Tier 3 Intensive Interventions?" (page 190). Discuss the first steps that can be taken to create a schoolwide identification, placement, and monitoring process. List these steps in area #4 of the PRTI Critical Steps to Success Chart.

5. Center Pyramid: Review the graphic organizer, and list 1 or 2 critical first steps from each of the surrounding boxes in the center pyramid. Determine a target date by which these steps are to be completed. These steps represent the short-term, high-leverage first steps that will be taken to create a PRTI.

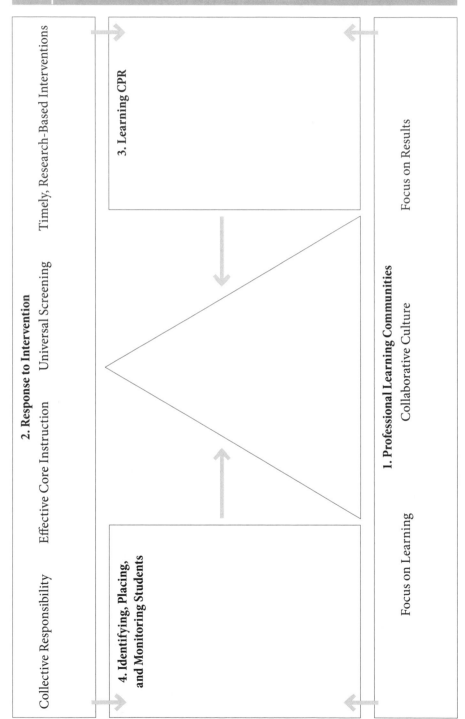

2. Response to Intervention

Collective Responsibility   Effective Core Instruction   Universal Screening   Timely, Research-Based Interventions

3. Learning CPR

4. Identifying, Placing, and Monitoring Students

1. Professional Learning Communities

Focus on Learning   Collaborative Culture   Focus on Results

PRTI Essential Standard Plan

This activity will help your team create a PRTI process to ensure that a group of students masters a specific, targeted essential standard.

1. Target Essential Skill/Standard: Using the format and essential questions from "Identifying Essential Standards" (page 177), identify the essential standard to be learned. To work best, this should be a high-leverage, essential standard.

2. Universal Screening: Record your responses to the following questions in the appropriate box on the form.

   - What skills or concepts related to the target standard should be measured prior to core instruction?

   - Who will administer the assessment?

   - When will the assessment be administered?

   - What assessment will be used?

   - Once the assessment was administered, what information was gained to help guide core instruction and preventive interventions?

3. Prior Skills Needed: Record your responses to the following questions in the appropriate box on the form.

   - What prior skills are needed by a student to have a high likelihood of mastering the targeted standard? (These skills can be measured in the universal screening tool.)

   - For students lacking in prerequisite skills, how and when will the skill(s) be taught to them prior to initial instruction on the targeted standard?

   - When will the assessment be administered?

   - What assessment will be used to measure student mastery of the prior skill(s)?

   - What research-based practices will be used to teach the prior skill(s)?

4. Tier 1 Core Instruction: Record your responses to the following questions in the appropriate box on the form.

   - What skills or concepts related to the target standard will be taught during the Tier 1 core instruction?

continued on page 198→

PRTI Essential Standard Plan (Cont'd)

- Who will teach the core instruction?

- When will the core instruction be taught?

- What formative common assessments will be used to measure student progress during core instruction?

- What research-based instructional practices will be used to teach the core instruction?

5. Tier 2 Supplemental Interventions: Record your responses to the following questions in the appropriate box on the form.

    - What interventions will be provided to intentional nonlearners and failed learners who did not demonstrate mastery after the Tier 1 core instruction?

    - Who will teach the interventions?

    - When will the interventions be offered?

    - What assessment(s) will be used to monitor student progress in each intervention?

    - What research-based instructional practices will be used for failed learners?

6. Tier 3 Intensive Interventions: Record your responses to the following questions in the appropriate box on the form.

    - What interventions will be provided to intentional nonlearners and failed learners who did not demonstrate mastery after Tier 2 supplemental interventions?

    - Who will teach the interventions?

    - When will the interventions be offered?

    - What assessment(s) will be used to monitor student progress in each intervention?

    - What research-based instructional practices will be used for failed learners?

Essential Standard Plan

Grade Level: _____ Subject: _____ Team Members: _____

Target Essential Skill/Standard: _____

	Administered By / Taught By	Administered When / Taught When	Assessment Tool / Assessment Tool for Progress-Monitoring	Assessment Findings / Research-Based Instructional Practices to Be Used
Universal Screening	Administered By	Administered When	Assessment Tool	Assessment Findings
Prior Skills Needed (Prevention)	Taught By	Taught When	Assessment Tool	Research-Based Instructional Practices to Be Used
Tier 1 Core Instruction (Goal: 75%+ Proficient)	Taught By	Taught When	Assessment Tool for Progress-Monitoring	Research-Based Instructional Practices to Be Used
Tier 2 Supplemental Interventions	Taught By	Taught When	Assessment Tool for Progress-Monitoring	Research-Based Instructional Practices to Be Used
Failed Learners: Intentional Nonlearners:				
Tier 3 Intensive Interventions	Taught By	Taught When	Assessment Tool for Progress-Monitoring	Research-Based Instructional Practices to Be Used
Failed Learners: Intentional Nonlearners:				

Creating a PRTI

This activity will help your team create a visual that represents your pyramid response to intervention. Using the graphic organizer, record your answers to the following questions. You may find it helpful to start by writing individual interventions on sticky notes. This makes it easier to move interventions around the chart while discussing possibilities.

1. Universal Screening

   • What universal screening tools will be used to assess all students in reading, writing, and math?

   • Who will administer the assessment?

   • When will the assessment be administered?

2. Tier 1 Core Program

   • What research-based instructional practices/programs will be used in your Tier 1 core program?

   • How will Tier 1 instruction be differentiated to meet the individual needs of students?

   • What formative common assessments will be used to measure student progress during core instruction?

3. Student Identification Process and Progress Monitoring

   • How will students be identified for supplemental interventions?

   • What criteria will be used to place students in the appropriate intervention?

   • Who will place students in interventions? How often?

   • How will student progress be monitored? By whom?

continued on page 201→

Creating a PRTI (Cont'd)

4. Tier 2 Supplemental Interventions

   - What interventions will be provided to intentional nonlearners and failed learners who did not demonstrate mastery after the Tier 1 core instruction?

   - What assessment(s) will be used to monitor student progress in each intervention?

   - What research-based instructional practices will be used for failed learners?

5. Progress-Monitoring and Decision Protocols

   - How will students be identified for intensive interventions?

   - What criteria will be used to place students in the appropriate intervention?

   - Who will place students in interventions? How often?

   - How will student progress be monitored? By whom?

6. Tier 3 Intensive Interventions

   - What interventions will be provided to intentional nonlearners and failed learners who did not demonstrate mastery after Tier 2 supplemental interventions?

   - Who will teach the interventions?

   - When will the interventions be offered?

   - What assessment(s) will be used to monitor student progress in each intervention?

   - What research-based instructional practices will be used for failed learners?

7. Decision Protocol

   - How will students be identified for special education testing?

   - What criteria and assessment data will be used to make this determination?

   - Who will make this decision?

continued on page 202→

Creating a PRTI (Cont'd)

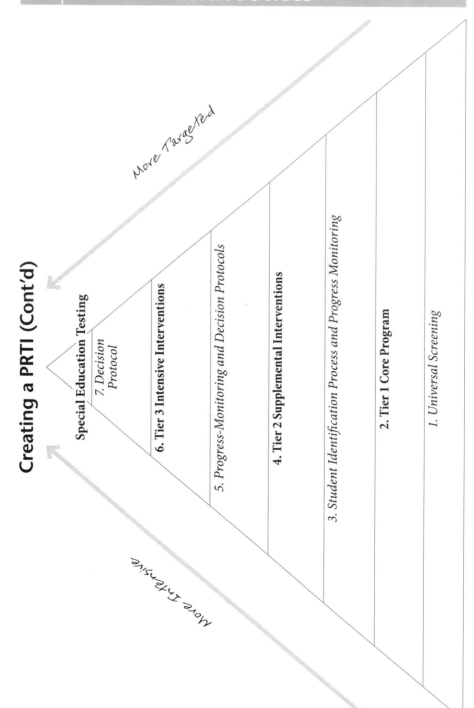

More Targeted

More Intensive

Special Education Testing

7. Decision Protocol

6. Tier 3 Intensive Interventions

5. Progress-Monitoring and Decision Protocols

4. Tier 2 Supplemental Interventions

3. Student Identification Process and Progress Monitoring

2. Tier 1 Core Program

1. Universal Screening

Sample Individualized Learning Plan (ILP)

A well-designed ILP records extensive data on a student, including DIBELS and QRI scores, results on district and state assessments, writing scores throughout the year, state English-language learner assessments, and information on the intervention programs in which the child is involved. Using a similar document, schools can record prior years' data and record the ongoing progress of students at risk.

Name _____

Grade _____ Birth _____

EL Level _____ Entry Date _____

DIBELS _____

Qualitative Reading Inventory _____

District Benchmark Tests

Reading _____

Mathematics _____

Language _____

State Tests

English Language Arts _____

Mathematics _____

Writing _____

English Learner Tests _____

Interventions

_____ begun on _____

_____ begun on _____

_____ begun on _____

_____ begun on _____

_____ begun on _____

_____ begun on _____

_____ begun on _____

Glossary

accommodation: A change made to instruction and/or assessment that does not change the content being measured or the rigor level required for the student to demonstrate proficiency.

adaptation: An adjustment to the instructional content or performance expectations for students with disabilities from what is expected or taught to students in the core program.

adequate yearly progress (AYP): The minimum student achievement levels schools are expected to make annually, according to an accountability system mandated by the No Child Left Behind Act of 2001, defined by individual states, and approved by the U.S. Department of Education.

aimline: A line on a graph that represents expected student progress over time.

cascade approach: Attributed to Stanley Deno, this term describes a continuum of five environments in which students with special needs can be served: homebound, special schools, self-contained classrooms, general education classrooms with pull-out support, and full inclusion in general education classrooms.

Collaborative Academic Support Teams (CAST): An RTI-like program in which classroom teachers and specialists provide support to small groups within the general education classroom. Students significantly below grade-level standards receive a replacement curriculum.

core curriculum: A basic course of study deemed critical and usually made mandatory for all students of a school or school system. Core curricula are often instituted by school boards, state departments of education, or other administrative agencies charged with overseeing education. Core curricula must be scientific and research-based.

criterion-referenced assessment: An assessment that measures what a student understands, knows, or can accomplish in relation to specific performance objectives rather than to other students' performance. (See also: *norm-referenced assessment*)

curriculum-based assessment (CBA): Measurement that uses direct observation and recording of a student's performance in the local curriculum as a basis for gathering information to make instructional decisions.

curriculum-based measurement (CBM): A precise tool for directly measuring student competency and progress in the basic skill areas of reading fluency, spelling, mathematics, and written language.

curriculum casualties: Students whose low achievement may be the result of poor instruction rather than of a learning disability.

data-based and data-driven decision-making: A continuous process of regularly collecting, summarizing, and analyzing information to guide development, implementation, and evaluation of an action; most importantly, this process is used to answer educational or socially important questions.

data points: Points on a graph that represent student achievement or behavior at a specific time relative to a specific assessment.

dependent variable: Any factor that may be influenced or modified by some treatment or exposure.

differentiated instruction: The process of designing lesson plans that meet the needs of the entire range of learners in the classroom; such planning includes learning objectives, grouping practices, teaching methods, varied assignments, and varied materials chosen based on student skill levels, interest levels, and learning preferences.

discrepancy: The difference between two outcome measures, as in the difference between pre- and post-test results on a criterion-referenced test. (See also: *IQ-achievement discrepancy*)

disproportionality: The over- or under-representation of students from a specific minority background in special education relative to the percentage of that minority in the general population.

early intervening services (EIS): Preventive intervention services for students in the early elementary grades that are designed to ameliorate their academic difficulties before referral to determine eligibility for special education becomes necessary; EIS is recommended by IDEIA 2004.

early literacy skills: The reading readiness abilities in letter naming and letter sounds upon which beginning reading is built.

early numeracy skills: The math readiness abilities in oral counting, number identification, and missing number recognition upon which beginning math is built.

English-language learner (ELL): A student whose home language is not English and who has not attained proficiency in English as measured by standardized tests.

evidence-based practice: Educational practices and instructional strategies supported by scientific research.

Excellence: A Commitment to Every Learner (ExCEL): An RTI-like program in which specialists provide small-group supplementary intervention to students when frequently given assessments reveal a need.

explicit instruction: A systematic instructional approach that includes a set of design and delivery procedures derived from effective schools research and behavior analysis; essential components of well-designed explicit instruction include a) implicit instructional design principles and assumptions that make up the content and strategies to be taught and b) visible delivery features of group instruction with a high level of teacher-student interaction.

fidelity: The degree of accuracy with which an intervention, program, or curriculum is implemented according to research findings and/or its developers' specifications.

formative assessment: Classroom and curriculum evaluations used to monitor student progress toward learning outcomes and to inform instructional decision-making.

functional analysis assessment (FAA): Assessments that use a variety of techniques to 1) diagnose the cause(s) of a behavior and 2) to identify interventions that might address the cause(s).

functional behavioral assessment (FBA): A process to identify a student's behavioral problem, determine its function or purpose, and develop interventions to teach acceptable alternate behaviors.

Heartland Area Education Agency (HAEA) model: An RTI-like program in which general and special educators work together to diagnose student needs, prescribe interventions, measure and monitor student progress, and adjust individualized student plans as needed.

Individuals with Disabilities Education Improvement Act of 2004 (IDEIA or IDEIA 2004): A federal statute, originally passed in 1975, that prescribes services to students aged 3–21 with disabilities.

inclusion: The policy of placing students with special needs in general education classes for the majority of the school day.

intensive intervention: An academic and behavioral intervention characterized by increased length, frequency, and duration of implementation and administered to students significantly below grade level; often associated with Tier 3, the narrowest tier of an RTI model; also referred to as *tertiary interventions*.

IQ-achievement discrepancy: The difference between scores on a norm-referenced intelligence test and a norm-referenced achievement test.

learning disability: See *specific learning disability*

learning rate: A student's average progress over a period of time.

Lexile levels: Numbers from 0 to 2,000 that denote both reading ability and text difficulty to help teachers identify a child's current reading level.

local education agency (LEA): A specific school district or a group of school districts in a cooperative or regional configuration.

No Child Left Behind (NCLB): Federal standards for students in elementary, middle, and high schools, as prescribed by the No Child Left Behind/Elementary and Secondary Education Act.

norm-referenced assessment: An assessment designed to discover how an individual student's performance or test result compares to that of an appropriate peer group. (See also: *criterion-referenced assessment*)

overidentification (over-representation): The assignment of more students to special education services than the state and national averages for special education assignment, or assignment of more students from a particular subgroup for such services than is proportionate to their presence in the general population.

positive behavior support (PBS): A tiered system of schoolwide practices that encourage and reward positive student and adult behavior.

power standards: A prioritized set of standards that require more attention or are more heavily represented on end-of-the-year tests, selected by determining which have the most endurance, leverage, and relevance for the next level of instruction.

probes: Brief, timed samples of a student's proficiency in reading, math, early literacy, or early numeracy, aligned to grade-level standards.

problem-solving approach: Assumes no given intervention will be effective for all students and is sensitive to individual student differences; generally has four stages (problem identification, problem analysis, plan implementation, and plan evaluation); success depends on the fidelity of implementing interventions.

problem-solving system: A form of RTI that utilizes staff
members' input and examines diagnosed student needs to formulate
individualized student plans.

problem-solving team: A group of education professionals who
collaboratively consider student-specific data, brainstorm possible
strategies and interventions, and develop a plan of action to address a
student-specific need.

progress monitoring: A scientifically based practice to assess
students' academic performance and evaluate the effectiveness of
instruction that can be used with individual students, a small group,
or an entire class. Also, the process used to monitor implementation
of specific interventions.

protocol system: A form of RTI in which students qualify for
intervention programs according to pre-established criteria and the
nature of their deficiencies.

pyramid of interventions (POI): A systematic program of
supports that become increasingly more directive, intensive, and
targeted. Named after the intervention program created at Adlai E.
Stevenson High in Lincolnshire, Illinois.

pyramid response to intervention (PRTI): The practice of
implementing the structures and procedures of response to intervention within the culture of a professional learning community; PRTI
combines the regulatory requirements of response to intervention with
the time-proven effectiveness of the pyramid of interventions.

research-based instruction: Curriculum and educational
interventions that have been scientifically proven to be effective for
most students.

response to intervention (RTI): The practice of providing high-
quality instruction and interventions matched to students' needs,
monitoring progress frequently to make changes in instruction or
goals, and applying child response data to important educational
decisions. (Also referred to as *response to instruction* or *responsiveness
to intervention*.)

scaffolding: An instructional technique in which the teacher breaks a complex task into smaller tasks, models the desired learning strategy or task, provides support as students learn to do the task, and then gradually shifts responsibility to the students. In this manner, a teacher enables students to accomplish as much of a task as possible without adult assistance.

specific learning disability (SLD): As defined by IDEIA 2004, a learning deficit in which the child, despite being provided with appropriate learning experiences and instruction, does not achieve adequately for the child's age or meet state-approved grade-level standards in one or more of the following areas: oral expression; listening comprehension; written expression; basic reading skills; reading fluency skills; reading comprehension; mathematics calculation; or mathematics problem-solving.

speech and language impairment (SLI): Problems in communication and related areas such as oral motor function.

student study team (SST): A group who meets regularly to recommend and implement strategies to assist students who are experiencing difficulties. The group may include administrators, teachers, psychologists, special education staff, and parents.

summative assessment: A comprehensive evaluation that measures a student's level of learning at the end of a unit of study.

supplementary intervention: Supports that augment primary instruction to directly address an area of need; often implemented in small-group settings but may be individualized; associated with Tier 2, the middle tier of an RTI model.

systematic data collection: A planned time frame for administering appropriate assessments to set baselines and monitor student progress.

systemic reform: Change that occurs in all aspects and levels of the educational process and that impacts all stakeholders within the process—students, teachers, parents, administrators, and community members—with implications for all components, including curriculum, assessment, professional development, instruction, and compensation.

Teaming for the Learning of all Children (TLC): An RTI-like program in which a team of specialists visits every grade level throughout the day to provide differentiated reading intervention to small groups of students.

tier: A level in a pyramid of interventions or an RTI system that includes interventions and supports for a clearly defined group of students.

tiered model: An educational model that delineates three or more levels of instructional interventions based on gaps in student skills.

Title I: The first major section of the No Child Left Behind Act, which funds and specifies compensatory programs for socioeconomically disadvantaged students.

trendline: A line on a graph that connects data points to compare a student's academic progress against his or her aimline to determine the student's responsiveness to intervention.

universal screening: A process of reviewing student performance through formal and/or informal assessment measures to determine progress in relation to student benchmarks and learning standards; also, the practice of assessing all students in a school with valid measures in the major curricular areas, so that no student at risk "falls through the cracks."

validated intervention: An intervention shown by educational research to be effective in meeting a set of identified student needs.

validity: An indication that an assessment instrument consistently measures what it is designed to measure.

References and Resources

Ainsworth, L., & Viegut, D. (2006). *Common formative assessments: How to connect standards-based instruction and assessment.* Thousand Oaks, CA: Corwin Press.

All Things Assessment. www.allthingsassessment.info

All Things PLC. www.allthingsplc.info

American Federation of Teachers. (2008). *Response to intervention.* Accessed at http://www.aft.org/topics/rti/index.htm on June 30, 2008.

Barth, R. S. (1990). *Improving schools from within: Teachers, parents, and principals can make a difference.* San Francisco: Jossey-Bass.

Barth, R. S. (2005). Turning book burners into lifelong learners. In R. DuFour, R. Eaker, & R. DuFour (Eds.), *On common ground: The power of professional learning communities* (pp. 115–134). Bloomington, IN: Solution Tree (formerly National Educational Services).

Batsche, G., Elliot, J., Graden, J. L., Grimes, J., Kovaleski, J. F., Prasse, D., Reschly, D. J., Schrag, J., & Tilly, III, W. D. (2006). *Response to intervention: Policy considerations and implementation.* Alexandria, VA: National Association of State Directors of Special Education, Inc.

Behavioral Interventions. Accessed at www.fsu.edu/~truancy/interventions.html on July 23, 2008.

Bergson, T. (2008). *Response to Intervention: Universal screening, progress monitoring, and model programs, policies and procedures.* Accessed at www.k12.wa.us/SpecialEd/RTI.aspx on April 22, 2008.

Bradley, R., Danielson, L. C., & Hallahan, D. P. (2002). *Identification of learning disabilities: Research to practice.* Washington, DC: Lawrence Erlbaum Associates.

Brown-Chidsey, R., & Steege, M. W. (2005). *Response to intervention: Principles and strategies for effective practice.* New York: Guilford Press.

Building the Legacy: IDEA 2004. Accessed at http://idea.ed.gov on July 23, 2008.

Burdette, P. (2007). *Response to intervention as it relates to early intervening services: Recommendations.* Accessed at www.projectforum.org/docs/ RtIasit RelatestoEIS.pdf on April 12, 2007.

California Department of Education. (2002). *Reading/language arts/ English language development adoption.* Accessed at www.cde.ca.gov/ ci/rl/im/rlaeld2002adoption.asp on June 11, 2007.

Caprara, G. V., Barbaranelli, C. P., Pastorelli, C., Bandura, A., & Zimbardo, P. G. (2000). Prosocial foundation of children's academic achievement. *Psychological Science, 11*(4) 302–306.

Carter, L. (2006). *Total instructional alignment: From stands to student success.* Bloomington, IN: Solution Tree.

Center for Effective Collaboration and Practice. Accessed at http://cecp. air.org/fba on July 23, 2008.

Chafouleas, S., Riley-Tilman, C., & Sugai, G. (2007). *School-based behavior assessment: Informing intervention and instruction.* New York: Guilford Press.

Collins, J. (2005a). *Good to great: Why some companies make the leap . . . and others don't.* New York: HarperCollins.

Collins, J. (2005b). Good to Great *and the social sectors: A monograph to accompany* Good to Great. Boulder, CO: Author.

Conzemius, A., & O'Neill, J. (2002). *The handbook for SMART school teams.* Bloomington, IN: Solution Tree (formerly National Educational Service).

Cook, C., & Sprague, J. (2008, May 6). *RTI for behavior: Applying RTI logic to ED eligibility.* Paper presented at LRP's National Institute on Legal Issues of Educating Individuals with Disabilities in Charlotte, NC.

Coordination Consultation & Evaluation Center. (n.d.) *K–3 reading and behavior interventions project.* Accessed at www.cce.wceruw.org on February 23, 2008.

Council for Exceptional Children. *Response-to-intervention—The promise and the peril.* Accessed at www.cec.sped.org/AM/Template.cfm? Section=Search&template=/CM/HTMLDisplay.cfm&Content ID=8427 on April 12, 2007.

Davies, A. (2007). Involving students in the classroom assessment process. In D. Reeves (Ed.), *Ahead of the curve: The power of assessment to transform teaching and learning* (pp. 31–57). Bloomington, IN: Solution Tree.

Deno, S. L. (2003). Development in curriculum-based measurement. *Journal of Special Education, 37*(3), 184–192.

Division for Learning Disabilities of the Council for Exceptional Children. (2006). *The role of the teacher of students with learning disabilities in the RTI process.* Accessed at www.TeachingLD.org/products/default.htm on June 1, 2007.

Drummond, T. (1993). *The student risk screening scale (SRSS).* Grants Pass, OR: Josephine County Mental Health Program.

Duffy, H. (2006). *Meeting the needs of significantly struggling learners in high school: A look at approaches to tiered intervention.* Washington, DC: American Institutes for Research, National High School Center.

DuFour, R. (2005). What is a professional learning community? In R. DuFour, R. Eaker, & R. DuFour (Eds.), *On common ground: The power of professional learning communities* (pp. 31–44). Bloomington, IN: Solution Tree (formerly National Educational Service).

DuFour, R., DuFour, R., Eaker, R., & Karhanek, G. (2004). *Whatever it takes: How professional learning communities respond when kids don't learn.* Bloomington, IN: Solution Tree (formerly National Educational Service).

DuFour, R., DuFour, R., Eaker, R., & Many, T. (2006). *Learning by doing: A handbook for professional learning communities at work*. Bloomington, IN: Solution Tree.

DuFour, R., & Eaker, R. (1998). *Professional learning communities at work: Best practices for enhancing student achievement*. Bloomington, IN: Solution Tree (formerly National Educational Service).

DuFour, R., DuFour, R., & Eaker, R. (2008). *Revisiting professional learning communities at work: New insights for improving schools*. Bloomington, IN: Solution Tree.

DuFour, R., Eaker, R., & DuFour, R. (2005a). Closing the knowing-doing gap. In R. DuFour, R. Eaker, & R. DuFour (Eds.), *On common ground: The power of professional learning communities* (pp. 225–252). Bloomington, IN: Solution Tree (formerly National Educational Service).

DuFour, R., Eaker, R., & DuFour, R. (2005b). Introduction. In R. DuFour, R. Eaker, & R. DuFour (Eds.), *On common ground: The power of professional learning communities* (pp. 1–6). Bloomington, IN: Solution Tree (formerly National Education Service).

DuFour, R., Eaker, R., & DuFour, R. (2005c). *On common ground: The power of professional learning communities*. Bloomington, IN: Solution Tree (formerly National Education Service).

DuFour, R., Eaker, R., & DuFour, R. (2005d). Recurring themes of professional learning communities and the assumptions they challenge. In R. DuFour, R. Eaker, & R. DuFour (Eds.), *On common ground: The power of professional learning communities* (pp. 7–30). Bloomington, IN: Solution Tree (formerly National Educational Service).

Eaker, R., DuFour, R., & DuFour, R. (2002). *Getting started: Reculturing schools to become professional learning communities*. Bloomington, IN: Solution Tree (formerly National Educational Service).

Eason-Watkins, B. (2005). Implementing PLCs in the Chicago Public Schools. In R. DuFour, R. Eaker, & R. DuFour (Eds.), *On common ground: The power of professional learning communities* (pp. 193–208). Bloomington, IN: Solution Tree (formerly National Educational Service).

Education Evolving. (2005). *Response to intervention: An alternative to traditional eligibility criteria for students with disabilities*. Accessed at www.educationevolving.org/pdf/Response_to_Intervention.pdf on April 12, 2007.

Education for All Handicapped Children Act of 1975, 20 U. S. C. Sec. 401 (1975).

Ehren, B. J., Montgomery, J., Rudebusch, J., & Whitmire, K. (2006). *Response to intervention: New roles for speech-language pathologists.* Rockville, MD: American Speech-Language Hearing Association.

Elliott, J. (2006, April 18). LD talk. [Interview.] Accessed at www.ncld.org/content/view/930 on November 17, 2007.

Faust, J. (2006, February). Response to intervention and problem solving: An administrator's perspective. *In Case: The News Letter for the Council of Administrators of Special Education, 47*(4), 1–2.

Feil, E. G., Severson, H. H., & Walker, H. M. (2002). Early screening and intervention to prevent the development of aggressive, destructive behavior patterns among at-risk children. In M.R. Shinn, H. M. Walker, and G. Stones (Eds.), *Interventions for academic and behavior problems II: Preventive and remedial approaches* (pp.143–160). Bethesda, MD: National Association of School Psychologists.

Feldman, K. (2007, June). *RTI—"Response to Intervention" and "Response to Instruction": Big ideas—big possibilities.* Paper presented at Orange County Department of Education, Costa Mesa, CA.

Fletcher, J. M., Coulter, W. A., Reschly, D. J., & Vaughn, S. (2004, December). Alternative approaches to the definition and identification of learning disabilities: Some questions and answers. *Annals of Dyslexia.* Accessed at http://findarticles.com/p/articles/mi_qa3809/is_200412/ai_n9471603/pg_4?tag=artBody;col1 on July 29, 2008.

Fletcher, J. M., & Denton, C. (2003, December). *Validity of alternative approaches to the identification of L .D.: Operationalizing unexpected underachievement.* Paper presented at the National Research Center on Learning Disabilities Responsiveness-to-Intervention Symposium, Kansas City, MO.

Florida Center for Reading Research. (2008). *Interventions for struggling readers.* Accessed at www.fcrr.org/Interventions/index.htm on April 22, 2008.

Fuchs, L. S., Deno, S. L., & Mirkin, P. K. (1984). The effects of frequent curriculum-based measurement and evaluation on pedagogy, student achievement, and student awareness of learning. *American Educational Research Journal, 21*(2), 449–460.

Fuchs, D., & Deschler, D. D. (2007). What we need to know about responsiveness to intervention (and shouldn't be afraid to ask). *Learning Disabilities Research & Practice, 22*, 129–136.

Fuchs, D., & Fuchs, L. S. (2005). Responsiveness to intervention: A blueprint for practitioners, policymakers, and parents. *Teaching Exceptional Children, 38*(1), 57–61.

Fuchs, L. S., & Fuchs, D. (2006). A framework for building capacity for responsiveness to intervention. *School Psychology Review, 35*(4), 621–626.

Fuchs, L. S., & Fuchs, D. (2007). A model for implementing responsiveness to intervention. *Teaching Exceptional Children, 39*(5), 14–20.

Fullan, M. (2005). Professional learning communities writ large. In R. DuFour, R. Eaker, & R. DuFour (Eds.), *On common ground: The power of professional learning communities* (pp. 209–224). Bloomington, IN: Solution Tree (formerly National Educational Service).

Gardner, J. (1988). *Leadership: An overview*. Washington, DC: Independent Sector.

Ginot, H. (1976). *Teacher and child*. New York: Avon Press.

Good, R. H., & Kaminski, R. A. (Eds.) (2002). *Dynamic indicators of basic early literacy skills* (6th ed.). Eugene, OR: Institute for the Development of Educational Achievement.

Gresham, F. M. (2004). Current status and future directions of school-based behavioral interventions. *School Psychology Review, 33*(3), 326–343.

Grimes, J., & Kurns, S. (2003, December). *An intervention-based system for addressing NCLB and IDEA expectations: A multiple tiered model to ensure every child learns*. Paper presented at the National Research Center on Learning Disabilities Responsiveness-to-Intervention Symposium, Kansas City, MO.

Guskey, Thomas (2007). Using assessments to improve teaching and learning. In D. Reeves (Ed.), *Ahead of the curve: The power of assessment to transform teaching and learning* (pp. 15–29). Bloomington, IN: Solution Tree.

Haigler, K. O., Harlow, C., O'Connor, P., & Campbell, A. (1994). *Literacy behind prison walls.* Washington, DC: National Center for Education Statistics.

Hawkins, J. D., Catalano, R. F., Kosterman, R., Abbott, R., & Hill, K. G. (1999). Preventing adolescent health-risk behaviors by strengthening protection during childhood. *Archives of Pediatrics & Adolescent Medicine, 153,* 226–234.

Hosp, J. L. (2006, May). Implementing RTI: Assessment practices and response to intervention. *National Association of School Psychologists Communique, 34*(7). Accessed at www.nasponline.org/publications/cq/cq347RTI.aspx.on November 20, 2007.

Individuals with Disabilities Education Act, 20 U. S. C. Sec. 1400 (1990).

Individuals with Disabilities Education Act, 20 U. S. C. Sec. 1400 (1997).

Individuals with Disabilities Education Improvement Act, 20 U. S. C. Sec. 1400 (2004).

International Dyslexia Association. (2006). *The role of reading intervention specialists in the RTI process.* Accessed at www.ira.org/downloads/resources/rti_role_definitions.pdf on June 1, 2007.

International Reading Association. (2006). *The role of reading specialists in the RTI process.* Accessed at www.ira.org/downloads/resources/rti_role_definitions.pdf on June 1, 2007.

Intervention Central. Accessed at www.interventioncentral.org on July 23, 2008.

Junger, S. (1997). *The perfect storm.* Boston: Little, Brown, and Co.

Kirsch, I., Braun, H., Yamamoto, K., & Sum, A. (2007). *America's perfect storm: Three forces changing our nation's future.* Princeton, NJ: Educational Testing Service. Accessed at www.ets.org/Media/Education_Topics/pdf/AmericasPerfectStorm.pdf on June 27, 2008.

Kirsch, I. S., Jungeblut, A., Jenkins, L., & Kolstad, A. (1993). *Adult literacy in America: A first look at the findings of the national adult literacy survey.* Washington, DC: National Center for Educational Statistics. Accessed at http://nces.ed.gov/pubs93/93275.pdf on June 27, 2008.

La Serna Bell Schedule. (1998). Accessed at www.wuhsd.k12.ca.us/811731025115952/blank/browse.asp?A=383&BMDRN=2000&BCOB=0&C=52590) on June 26, 2008.

Learning Disabilities Association of America. (2006). *The roles of parents/family in responsiveness to intervention.* Accessed at http://www.ira.org/downloads/resources/rti_role_definitions.pdf on June 1, 2007.

Levin, H., Belfield, C., Muenning, P., & Rouse, C. (2007). *The costs and benefits of an excellent education for all of America's children.* Accessed at http://www.cbcse.org/media/download_gallery/Leeds_Report_Final_Jan2007.pdf on March 17, 2007.

Lezotte, L. W. (2005). More effective schools: Professional learning communities in action. In R. DuFour, R. Eaker, & R. DuFour (Eds.), *On common ground: The power of professional learning communities* (pp. 177–192). Bloomington, IN: Solution Tree (formerly National Educational Service).

Managing On-site Discipline for Effective Learning. Accessed at www.modelprogram.com/?pageid=41897 on July 23, 2008.

Marzano, R. (2003). *What works in schools: Translating research into action.* Alexandria, VA: Association for Supervision and Curriculum Development.

McCook, J. E. (2006). *The RTI guide: Developing and implementing a model in your schools.* Horsham, PA: LRP Publications.

Moller, S., & Stearns, E. (2004). *Retention and school dropout: Examining connectivity between children and schools.* Paper presented at the annual meeting of the American Sociological Association, San Francisco, CA, August 14. Accessed at http://www.allacademic.com/meta/p108764_index.html on April 22, 2008.

National Association of State Directors of Special Education / Council of Administrators of Special Education. (2006). Response to intervention: NASDSE and CASE White Paper on RTI. Accessed at http://www.

nasdse.org/Portals/0/Documents/Download%20Publications/ RtIAnAdministratorsPerspective1-06.pdf on June 1, 2007.

National Association of School Psychologists. (2006). *The role of the school psychologist in the RTI process.* Accessed at http://www.ira.org/ downloads/resources/rti_role_definitions.pdf on June 1, 2007.

National Center for Learning Disabilities. (1999, May 6–7). Summit on research in learning disabilities: Keys to successful learning. Washington, DC.

National Center for Learning Disabilities. (2006). *Response to intervention.* Accessed at www.ira.org/downloads/resources/rti_role_definitions.pdf on June 1, 2007.

National Education Association. (2006). *The role of general education teachers in the RTI process.* Accessed at www.ira.org/downloads/ resources/rti_role_definitions.pdf on June 1, 2007.

National Institute of Child Health and Human Development. (2000). *Report of the National Reading Panel: Teaching children to read (00–4769).* Washington, DC: U.S. Government Printing Office.

National Research Center on Learning Disabilities. (2006a, Spring). *RTI manual.* Washington, DC: Author.

National Research Center on Learning Disabilities. (2006b, Spring). *Tiered service delivery: Rosewood Elementary School, Vero Beach, Florida.* Accessed at www.nrcld.org/rti_practices/tiers/rosewood.html on June 30, 2008.

National Technical Assistance Center on Positive Behavior Interventions and Support. Accessed at www.pbis.org on July 23, 2008.

No Child Left Behind Act of 2001, Public Law 107-110, 5, 115 Stat. 1427 (2002), et seq.

O'Connor, K. (2007). The last frontier: Tackling the grading dilemma. In D. Reeves (Ed.), *Ahead of the curve: The power of assessment to transform teaching and learning* (pp. 127–145). Bloomington, IN: Solution Tree.

Oregon Department of Education. (2007). *Oregon's Response to Intervention initiative.* Accessed at http://ode.state.or.us/initiatives/idea.RTI.aspx on June 8, 2007.

President's Commission on Excellence in Special Education. (2002). *A new era: Revitalizing special education for children and their families.* Accessed at www.ed.gov/inits/commissionsboards/whspecialeducation/ on May 25, 2007.

Public Law 94–142, *Education of the Handicapped Act of 1975. Federal Register,* 42, 163, (August 23, 1977).

Reeves, D. (2000). *Accountability in action: A blueprint for learning organizations.* Denver, CO: Advanced Learning Press.

Reeves, D. (2004). *101 Questions & answers about standards, assessment, and accountability.* Englewood, CO: Advanced Learning Press.

Reeves, D. (2005). Putting it all together: Standards, assessment, and accountability in successful professional learning communities. In R. DuFour, R. Eaker, & R. DuFour (Eds.), *On common ground: The power of professional learning communities* (pp. 45–64). Bloomington, IN: Solution Tree (formerly National Educational Service).

Reeves, D. (Ed.) (2007). *Ahead of the curve: The power of assessment to transform teaching and learning.* Bloomington, IN: Solution Tree.

Reschly, D. (2005). Learning disabilities: Primary intervention, secondary intervention, and then what? *Journal of Learning Disabilities, 38*(6), 510–515.

Roberts, L. (1998). *Illiteracy on the rise in America.* Accessed at www. wsws.org/news/1998/oct1998/ill-o14.shtml on February 14, 2008.

Rubin, R. (2006, January 24). We must change policy direction. *Wall Street Journal,* p. A-20.

Sadler, C., & Zinn, P. (2005, July). *Early intervention/RtI in Tigard-Tualatin school district: Effective behavior & instructional support* (EBIS). Presentation made at Office of Special Education Program's Project Directors Conference, Washington, DC.

Sandomierski, T., Kincaid, D., & Algozzine, B. (2007). Response to intervention and positive behavior support: Brothers from different mothers or sisters from different misters? *Positive Behavioral Interventions and Supports Newsletter, 4*(2), 1–4.

Saphier, J. (2005). Masters of motivation. In R. DuFour, R. Eaker, & R. DuFour (Eds.), *On common ground: The power of professional learning communities* (pp. 85–114). Bloomington, IN: Solution Tree (formerly National Educational Service).

Scherer, M. (2001, September). How and why standards can improve student achievement: A conversation with Robert J. Marzano. *Educational Leadership, 59*(1), 14–18.

Schlechty, P. C. (1997). *Inventing better schools.* San Francisco: Jossey-Bass.

Schmoker, M. (2001). *Results fieldbook: Practical strategies from dramatically improved schools.* Alexandria, VA: Association for Supervision and Curriculum Development.

Schmoker, M. (2005). No turning back: The ironclad case for professional communities. In R. DuFour, R. Eaker, & R. DuFour (Eds.), *On common ground: The power of professional learning communities* (pp. 135–154). Bloomington, IN: Solution Tree (formerly National Educational Service).

Schoolwide Information System. Accesed at www.swis.org on July 23, 2008.

Senge, P. (1990). *The fifth discipline: The art and practice of the learning organization.* New York: Currency Doubleday.

Shaywitz, S. (2003). *Overcoming dyslexia.* New York: Random House.

Sparks, D. (2005). Leading for transformation in teaching, learning, and relationships. In R. DuFour, R. Eaker, & R. DuFour (Eds.), *On common ground: The power of professional learning communities* (pp. 155–174). Bloomington, IN: Solution Tree (formerly National Educational Service).

Stiggins, R. (2005). Assessment for learning: Building a culture of confident learners. In R. DuFour, R. Eaker, & R. DuFour (Eds.), *On common ground: The power of professional learning communities* (pp. 65–84). Bloomington, IN: Solution Tree (formerly National Educational Service).

Stiggins, R. J., Arter, J. A., Chappuis, J., & Chappuis, S. (2004). *Classroom assessment for student learning: Doing it right—using it well.* Portland, OR: ETS Assessment Training Institute.

Stiggins, R., Chappuis, S., Arter, J., & Chappuis, J. (2004). *Assessment for learning: An action guide for school leaders.* Portland, OR: ETS Assessment Training Institute.

Sugai, G. (2007, December). *RTI: Reasons, practices, systems, and considerations.* Paper presented at Response to Intervention Summit, Washington, D.C.

Sugai, G., & Horner, R. R. (2006). A promising approach for expanding and sustaining schoolwide positive behavior support. *School Psychology Review, 35*(2), 245–259.

Sum, A., Kirsch, I., & Yamamoto, K. (2004). *A human capital concern: The literacy proficiency of U.S. immigrants.* Princeton, NJ: Educational Testing Service.

Tilly, III, W. D. (2006, Winter/Spring). Response to intervention: An overview. What is it? Why do it? Is it worth it? *The Special EDge, 19*(2), 1–3.

Tomlinson, C. A. (1999). *The differentiated classroom: Responding to the needs of all learners.* Alexandria, VA: Association for Supervision and Curriculum Development.

Torgesen, J. K., Alexander, A. W., Wagner, R. K., Rashotte, C. A., Voeller, K. K. S., & Conway, T. (2001). Intensive remedial instruction for children with severe reading disabilities: Immediate and long-term outcomes from two instructional approaches. *Journal of Learning Disabilities, 34,* 33–58.

Usaj, K., Shine, J. K., & Mandlawitz, M. (2006). *Response to intervention: New roles for school social workers.* Accessed at www.ira.org/downloads/resources/rti_role_definitions.pdf on June 1, 2007.

U.S. Department of Education. (2008). *Building the legacy: IDEA 2004.* Accessed at http://Idea.ed.gov/ on May 19, 2008.

U.S. Department of Education. (2005, June 21). Assistance to states for the education of children with disabilities. *Federal Register, 70*(118). Accessed at http://www.ed.gov/legislation/FedRegister/proprule/2005-2/062105a.html on July 30, 2008.

U.S. Department of Education's Institute of Education Sciences (2008). *What works clearinghouse.* Accessed at http://ies.ed.gov/ncee/wwc/ on November 13, 2007.

U.S. Office of Special Education. (2008). National Technical Assistance Center on Positive Behavioral Interventions and Supports (PBIS). Accessed at www.pbis.org/main.htm on February 23, 2008.

Vaughn, S., & Roberts, G. (2007). Secondary interventions in reading: Providing additional instruction for students at risk. *Teaching Exceptional Children, 39*(5), 40.

Vaughn Gross Center for Reading and Language Arts. (2005). *Introduction to the 3-tier reading model: Reducing reading difficulties for kindergarten through third grade students* (4th ed.). Austin: University of Texas, Vaughn Gross Center for Reading and Language Arts.

Washington Department of Education, Office of Superintendent of Public Instruction. (2006). *Using Response to Intervention (RTI) for Washington's students.* Accessed at www.k12.wa.us/SpecialEd/RTI. aspx on June 8, 2007.

Wedgeworth, R. (2003). *The number of functionally illiterate adults is growing.* Accessed at www.proliteracy.org/downloads/ ProLiteracyStateOfLiteracy%2010–25–04.pdf on May 18, 2008.

Wright, D. B., Cafferata, G., Keller, D., & Saren, D. (2007). *The BSP Desk Reference: A teacher and behavior support team's guide to developing and evaluating behavior support plans.* Accessed at www.pent.ca.gov on February 27, 2008.

Revisiting Professional Learning Communities at Work™

Richard DuFour, Rebecca DuFour, and Robert Eaker

This 10th-anniversary sequel to *Professional Learning Communities at Work™* offers advanced insights on deep implementation, the commitment/consensus issue, and the human side of PLC. **BKF252**

Understanding Response to Intervention

Robert Howell, Sandra Patton, and Margaret Deiotte

This straightforward book delivers the nuts and bolts of RTI. Clear examples of effective practices include systems and checklists to assess your RTI progress. **BKF253**

The Collaborative Administrator

Austin Buffum, Cassandra Erkens, Charles Hinman, Susan Huff, Lillie G. Jessie, Terri L. Martin, Mike Mattos, Anthony Muhammad, Peter Noonan, Geri Parscale, Eric Twadell, Jay Westover, and Kenneth C. Williams

Foreword by Robert Eaker

Introduction by Richard DuFour

In a culture of shared leadership, the administrator's role is more important than ever. This book addresses your toughest challenges with practical strategies and inspiring insight. **BKF256**

Raising the Bar and Closing the Gap: Whatever It Takes

Richard DuFour, Rebecca DuFour, Robert Eaker, and Gayle Karhanek

This sequel to the best-selling *Whatever It Takes: How Professional Learning Communities Respond When Kids Don't Learn* expands on original ideas and presses further with new insights. **BKF378**

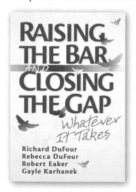

Solution Tree | Press

Visit solution-tree.com or call 800.733.6786 to order.